The SCRUM Fieldbook

The SCRUM Fieldbook

A Master Class on Accelerating Performance, Getting Results, and Defining the Future

J. J. Sutherland

CURRENCY
NEW YORK

Copyright © 2019 by J. J. Sutherland and Scrum Inc.

All rights reserved.
Published in the United States by Currency, an imprint of Random House, a division of Penguin Random House LLC, New York.
currencybooks.com

CURRENCY and its colophon are trademarks of Penguin Random House LLC.

Currency books are available at special discounts for bulk purchases for sales promotions or corporate use. Special editions, including personalized covers, excerpts of existing books, or books with corporate logos, can be created in large quantities for special needs. For more information, contact Premium Sales at (212) 572-2232 or e-mail specialmarkets@penguinrandomhouse.com.

Library of Congress Cataloging-in-Publication Data

Names: Sutherland, J. J., author.
Title: The Scrum fieldbook: a master class on accelerating performance, getting results, and defining the future / J. J. Sutherland.
Description: New York: Currency, [2019] | Includes bibliographical references and index.
Identifiers: LCCN 2019004437 | ISBN 9780525573210
Subjects: LCSH: Organizational change. | Organizational effectiveness.
Classification: LCC HD58.8 .S8826 2019 | DDC 658.4/06—dc23 LC record available at https://lccn.loc.gov/2019004437

Hardcover ISBN 978-0-525-57321-0
International edition ISBN 978-0-593-13745-1
Ebook ISBN 978-0-525-57322-7

PRINTED IN THE UNITED STATES OF AMERICA

Book design by Andrea Lau

10 9 8 7 6 5 4 3 2 1

First Edition

for v*

for insisting the book's bedrock be joy
por exigir que el poste estrella del libro siempre sea esperanza
for declaring you married a writer
para enamorarte de mi otra vez
for the constant reminder to look to the light
Estoy muy bendecido y agradecido de tenerte en mi vida
This book would not be what it is without you

CONTENTS

CHAPTER 1	The Choice Before Us	3
CHAPTER 2	Making It Cheap to Change Your Mind	22
CHAPTER 3	Why We Can't Decide	39
CHAPTER 4	Busy vs. Done	68
CHAPTER 5	People and Places That Seem Crazy Usually Are	87
CHAPTER 6	Structure Is Culture	117
CHAPTER 7	Doing It Right	149
CHAPTER 8	What Not to Do	180
CHAPTER 9	The Renaissance Enterprise	207
CHAPTER 10	The Way the World Could Be	227
ACKNOWLEDGMENTS		241
NOTES		245
INDEX		249

THE
SCRUM
FIELDBOOK

CHAPTER 1

The Choice Before Us

One of the most exciting things about life to me is the frequent discovery that the way I thought the world worked isn't, in fact, the way the world works. I find the revelation of just how mistaken I am to be thrilling. It implies that there is a fresher, better, more accurate, and more encompassing way of seeing the world. I have been given the gift of realizing that my old axioms, my old locked-in ways of understanding how things worked, were wrong. Usually I find that the way things work in biology, in science, in business, and in life is more intricate and involved, more subtle, and more open to change than I ever imagined. It's incredibly freeing.

It reminds me of the story behind the publication of Antoine Lavoisier's revolutionary book *Traité élémentaire de chimie* (*Elements of Chemistry*) in 1789. Lavoisier proposed that through rigorous experimentation one could derive basic principles:

> It is a maxim universally admitted in geometry, and indeed in every branch of knowledge, that, in the progress of inves-

tigation, we should proceed from known facts to what is unknown. . . . In this manner, from a series of sensations, observations, and analyses, a successive train of ideas arises, so linked together, that an attentive observer may trace back to a certain point the order and connection of the whole sum of human knowledge.[1]

Lavoisier theorized that there were basic chemical elements that could not be broken down. He argued that they formed the building blocks of matter. And so he rigorously began to seek them out. He's the scientist who named oxygen, hydrogen, and carbon, the person who discovered oxygen's role in combustion and respiration, who showed that water is made up of hydrogen and oxygen. He revolutionized the field of chemistry. He created a whole new language to describe how the component parts of reality interact with each other. In other words, he described anew how the world works. He was able to use the basic principles he set out to predict the existence of other elements that weren't discovered in his lifetime.

Before Lavoisier, chemists could only examine those chemicals that nature just happened to have left lying around. Lavoisier's idea was that instead of just limiting ourselves to those elements, why not experiment until we can find the entire universe of all possible chemical compounds, not just those that we conveniently stumble upon?

His ideas were stunning. The publication of his book became one of the great dividing lines in the history of science. Before Lavoisier, scientists and intellectuals assumed the world worked one way. After, it was understood that the world worked completely differently. Modern chemistry was born. The world had fundamentally shifted. Today, everything from the buttons on your shirt to the chill of your refrigerator to the ink in this book or the very chips driving the device in your hands as you read these words is there only because of that discovery.

I love it when that kind of thing happens. When a new discovery fundamentally changes how we view and understand the world we live in. When everything we thought we knew is thrown into question, because of new information or new data. When the world was one way one day, and the next we have possibilities we weren't even capable of conceiving the day before.

A New Way of Thinking

In the years since the publication of my first book, *Scrum: The Art of Doing Twice the Work in Half the Time*, co-authored with my father, Jeff Sutherland, more and more people are waking up to the fact that we are in the midst of a similar change in how the world of business works now. A revolution is driving change in the business world. And, as with Lavoisier's work, it is showing us a new world, where the old limits don't even apply. I've been using a new phrase recently in my conversations with companies, CEOs, and senior executives: Scrum is the art of changing the *possible*.

The need for Scrum is being driven by rapid social, economic, and political changes, which in turn are being driven by the immense speed of technological advances. You've no doubt heard of Moore's law, coined by Gordon Moore, the co-founder of Intel. In 1965 he wrote a paper with the joyful title "Cramming More Components onto Integrated Circuits." What is now called Moore's law is the conclusion of the paper: the number of transistors on a chip would double every two years. That's exponential growth. Oh, and the price of that increased computing power is cut in half at the same time.

We cannot even perceive how fast that rate of change is. It is becoming impossible to wrap your head around what will come next. Let me share an old French children's riddle to illustrate just how fast things are taking place. Let's say you come across a beautiful lily pond—maybe the one in Giverny made so famous by Monet's dozens of paintings. Picture it in your head. Still water, lilies floating on the surface, maybe a small bridge, the sky and the trees framing the pond, painting it with their reflections.

Now let's say the number of lilies in the pond doubles every day. Thirty days from now they will completely cover the surface of the water, smothering the pond with petals. The lilies, through no fault of their own, will kill all other life in the pond—fish, frogs, even the lilies themselves. But there is time, isn't there, to save the pond? And after all, the lilies are lovely. If you decide to wait to intervene until the lilies cover half the pond, how many days will you have to save the pond?

One. Just one. On day twenty-nine the lilies will cover half the pond. The next day they will cover the whole thing.

Let me offer another example of the pace a doubling of transistors and power brings about. Let's use the famous example of grains of wheat on a chessboard, which dates back to 1256 (giving you some indication of how long people have been thinking about this sort of thing). If you were to place one grain of wheat on one square of a chessboard and then in each succeeding square double the number of grains of wheat, by the time you got to the last square on the board you would have doubled sixty-three times. That last square would have some 9 *quintillion* (9,223,372,036,854,775,808 to be precise) grains of wheat. That is a big, big number. Incomprehensible. Unfathomable. And that is the rate of change we are living through. The old ways of working are breaking down when faced with rapidly changing problems that are simply beyond their capability of addressing. Complexity is no longer a rarity; it is something we must grapple with every day.

What Happens After What Comes Next

Scrum is a way for a person, a team, or an organization to be able to respond to that complexity, to respond to change that cannot be predicted, to move nimbly with alacrity through a constantly changing problem space. The sheer pace of the changes we are living through demands a different way of working. Scrum is an answer to that problem.

But to truly get the power of Scrum, the kind of dramatic productivity and value delivery increases it provides, there has to be a fundamental change in management and operations. While a few Scrum Teams can get things out the door with remarkable speed, what you really want is Scrum at the enterprise level. The traditional structures have to change, the incentives have to change, performance management has to change, and people across the organization, even if they aren't on Scrum Teams themselves, have to learn how to interact with, supply, help, and manage those Teams in a new way.

People in traditional organizations, once they really grasp the size of the change necessary, sometimes just throw their hands up. It's impossible. It's too big a leap. There is too much bureaucracy, too much history, too many corporate "ways of doing things" in established companies. *We can't just change everything,* managers say; *that's just not how we work around here.* And if things go wrong, they start looking around for someone to blame.

It doesn't matter who was responsible for a company's success or failure, or how the money was spent, or what went wrong. The only thing that matters is: what happens after what comes next? The past is the past. This is true in business, politics, or relationships. What do you want the future to look like? How can you position yourself to take advantage of the changes you know are needed? How do you build into your team, division, or company not simply resiliency but a system that actually helps the team grow stronger each time a problem is encountered? How do we build a system robust enough that every time a disaster strikes, it not only recovers but grows, learns, and becomes more capable?

The best organizations learn from their mistakes and successes and then systematically use those lessons to get better. As I often tell my Teams when they bring me something that failed, "Great. Now we know that doesn't work. Next time, bring me a more interesting mistake."

What you really want is what I call a Renaissance Enterprise—one that has freed itself from the shackles of the past, from the old ways of looking at the world, and is now capable of creating things that were unimaginable just a few years ago. We need a Moore's law for people. How do we get faster and more efficient and productive ourselves? And how do we do it at scale?

A World Made of Lego

Come with me to northern Europe, to Sweden—the home of Ikea, *The Girl with the Dragon Tattoo*, the pop band ABBA, possibly the world's premier meatballs, and the midnight sun. Sweden is also home to Saab. You might know Saab as a car manufacturer that no longer makes cars, but making cars was always a sideline for the company. What Saab is really about is making fighter planes. Who knew?

Saab has been building fighters for decades, going back to 1937. It was obvious at the time that the world was about to enter a worldwide conflagration, and Sweden, not closely aligned to any party or country, decided to build its own air force. The country has had an official policy of neutrality, similar to Switzerland's, since the end of the Napoleonic Era. And it was able to maintain that policy, officially, through World War II and the Cold War. But having NATO on one side and the USSR on the other was, shall we say, a stressful situation for our good friends in the Elongated Country.

So the Swedes built themselves an air force. In 1950 they introduced the Saab 29 Tunnan fighter, a fighter on par with the best fighter jets in the world at the time. They built some fifty-five operational squadrons, many standing by on alert and able to be launched in sixty seconds. In time they began selling their airplanes to other countries: Austria, Brazil, South Africa, Thailand, and others.

After Tunnan came the Lansen, the Draken, and then, in the 1980s, the Gripen A/B, followed by the C/D. And then they had a problem. The Gripen was a good plane and sold pretty well. But Saab, and the Swedish military, wanted to modernize it, make it more powerful, give it a longer range and better weapons. And that is how the idea for the Gripen E came about. At first the engineers at Saab were simply going to modernize sixty or so existing Gripen 39Cs, because, hey, planes are expensive and hard to build. Eventually, while they were updating the planes, they adopted Scrum—at first only in their software group, but it soon began to spread: to design, engineering, quality, everywhere. Scrum@Scale is a modular organizational framework, with cross-functional Teams delivering value quickly. But as it spread through Saab, the company's leaders had a radical new idea—what if the plane reflected the firm's organizational structure?

We want an aircraft that can potentially fly for fifty years, Saab pointed out. *We know the technology will radically change over the decades. Current aircraft designs are really hard to update. They're tightly coupled. Each piece entangled with every other. What if we build a plane that is modular, that can easily be taken apart and put back together, just like an organization of Scrum Teams? We could update whole systems all the time. We wouldn't have to wait for a whole new modernization program.*

Instead, why not make it so that if new radar or new computers or a better engine comes out, we can just take out the old one and plug in the new one, without having to touch the rest of the plane? What if we built a fighter plane as if it was built out of Lego?

"We want it to be a plug-and-play system," said Saab's Jorgen Furuhjelm. "We call it a smart fighter. We don't know what our customers will want in a few years."

Need to develop a better engine? No problem—just swap it out. Improved radar? Done. Niftier weapons? Sorted. The Saab philosophy allows the Gripen to do things that would seem impossible. It can land on a road in extreme weather conditions. It can be refueled and rearmed in under ten minutes—you only need six people and no special tools. Most other fighters take two to three times that long. Saab can swap an engine out in an hour. That's what modularity does for you.

And the company is a *fun* place to work. Swedish engineering students rank only Google higher as the best place to work. And unlike most companies in the world, where most people would rather be doing almost anything else than going to the office, employees *want* to go to work every day at Saab.

"It's about commitment. People think the project is cool. Really cool. They're into planes. And there is this sense of *commitment* on the Teams you can almost touch," says Furuhjelm.

That's the power of Scrum. It frees people up to work faster, to work more productively, and to accomplish more work in less time. It allows Teams to pursue their work with passion and without impediments. When Saab embraced Scrum, they discovered that by simply focusing on getting things out of people's way, they could unleash a staggering amount of human potential.

Even though the Gripen E is just better, with better parts and better equipment—better just about everything—than its predecessor, the plane is cheaper to develop, cheaper to build, and cheaper to operate. To keep 150 Gripens in the air for forty years would cost you about $22 billion. That's about half of what it would cost to keep just 65 American-built F35s aloft.

And they did it with Scrum. Built a highly advanced fighter from the ground up. There are a lot of times when I'm working at companies whose managers say, *Oh, the Scrum framework is designed for creating software. What we are doing is far too complex to be Agile.* That's usually when I start to tell them about the Gripen. "I'm pretty sure," I say, "that whatever you are making or building, it's not more complicated than a fighter plane."

I'm Not Sure That Word Means What You Think It Does

In recent years Scrum, often under the banner of Agile, has become ubiquitous. It's no longer just the way software and technology companies work, but the way large companies increasingly work in almost every domain. Companies that specialize in banking, automobiles, medical devices, biotech, insurance, healthcare, and others have turned to Agile as a way of staying relevant today. Blue chip companies like Bosch, Coca-Cola, USAA, Schlumberger, Fidelity, and Lockheed Martin have all turned to Scrum to deliver the value and quality at the speed their customers are now saying is simply required.

Much of this has been driven by what are often called digital transformations. The idea is that the old days of a separation between business and IT are gone for good. Nowadays every company is a technology company. And software has eaten the world. There are more lines of code in your car than there are in Windows. Heck, my new washing machine wants the Wi-Fi password.

And now companies—often spurred by a CEO who saw a TED Talk or heard about the benefits of Agile from their peers or a consulting company—decide that, come hell or high water, will become Agile.

At this point, I think it would help for me to define the term *Agile*, and how Scrum relates to it. Scrum was invented in 1993, and then formalized by its two co-creators, Jeff Sutherland and Ken Schwaber, in 1995. Throughout the mid-1990s, on Usenet groups and at conferences, there were many people who were struggling to come up with ways of developing software that wouldn't have the horrible failure rate that was becoming more and more common.

In 2001, seventeen of those people got together at a ski resort in Snowbird, Utah, for a couple of days. My father, Jeff Sutherland, was there, as were Ken Schwaber and another early adopter of Scrum, Mike Beedle. The fourteen other people came from different backgrounds and methodologies, but they recognized that they were all attempting to address the same problems in ways that were similar, if not precisely the same.

The first day, as I've been told the story by a few people who were there, they argued. They mainly argued about what they were going to call this umbrella that they knew was there but didn't have a name for. Near the end of the day, Mike Beedle suggested the name Agile. Everyone thought that would be an easier sell than some of the runners-up, like Lightweight. So they decided to call it Agile. Then they started to debate what that meant.

The next day they argued some more. Okay, it was Agile, but what did that actually mean? How could it be described? Well, nine of the people in the room decided to take a smoke break, while the other eight stayed inside. One of them, Martin Fowler, went up to the whiteboard and said something along the lines of, *Wouldn't it be a shame if we couldn't agree on something during these two days?* In about fifteen minutes the eight people in that room came up with this:

We are uncovering better ways of developing software by doing it and helping others do it. Through this work we have come to value:

Individuals and interactions over processes and tools

Working software over comprehensive documentation

Customer collaboration over contract negotiation

Responding to change over following a plan

That is, while there is value in the items on the right, we value the items on the left more.

Fifteen minutes later when the other nine people came back in the room, one of them, Ward Cunningham—the inventor of the wiki, among other things—said, "That's awesome!" Not a word was changed.

So that's Agile. It's a statement of values. They spent the rest of the day coming up with twelve principles like "Simplicity—the art of maximizing the amount of work not done—is essential," and "Build projects around motivated individuals. Give them the environment and support they need, and trust them to get the job done," and "Continuous attention to technical excellence and good design enhances agility." All great things, but not a description of how to actually do them. There was no framework, no methodology, just four values and some pretty commonsense principles.

And it changed the world. They put the Agile Manifesto up on a website, agilemanifesto.org, and went home to continue the hard work of actually doing it. They had no idea of the impact it would have far beyond the world of software.

But I do want to caution you that when anyone says they are Agile, it's really important to ask them what exactly they mean by that. Scrum is by far the most popular way to do it—some 70 percent of Agile teams use Scrum. It isn't the only way by any means, but just saying a company is Agile doesn't tell you a whole lot.

Moore's Law for People

If you've never heard of Scrum before, or even if you've been introduced to it but still aren't sure how it can help your business, let me give you a quick history lesson on where Scrum comes from and what it set out to do.

People in Silicon Valley have been concerned about the impact of Moore's law on the rapid growth of technology since the late 1980s. As the machines we built became capable of doing more, software projects became more complex, and, sadly, failure of those projects became more common, wasting ever larger amounts of time, energy, productivity, and dreams.

Let's take the TAURUS project at the London Stock Exchange around this time. TAURUS is an acronym for Transfer and Automated Registration of Uncertified Stock. The problem was, the settlements system at the exchange used a system called Talisman. *Settlements* is a fancy word for "getting what you paid for." So after you bought a stock on the exchange, actually getting that stock transferred to your portfolio could take two to three weeks, and it involved shipping actual paper stock certificates from one place to another. The dealing system, the buying and selling of bit, was called Seaq. It was electronic, but it couldn't talk to the Talisman system, which predated it by many years.

TAURUS was supposed to fix that. It was an electronic settlements system that would replace the old paper system, and also tie into international settlements systems to allow trading of international securities. It would be awesome. But individual traders needed one thing, wholesalers another. Most traders also wanted

TAURUS to talk to their custom systems, not replace them. So more and more requirements began to be tacked onto the TAURUS program.

Still, it was going to be awesome. It would integrate with some seventeen different systems. Amazing. The problem, according to Hamish McRae, writing in the *Independent* on March 12, 1993, was threefold. First, trying to build huge software systems from scratch and launching it in one "Big Bang" is incredibly risky. There can be no small failures or mistakes. The smallest of failures would be catastrophic. Yet this approach was commonplace at the time, and it's sometimes seen even today. Companies place huge bets that some massive system will fix everything right out of the gate. According to data from the Standish Group, about 40 percent of projects working this way are total failures.[2] Half of them are late, are over budget, and don't deliver what they were intended to do. For TAURUS, those were long odds for a system that was supposed to completely replace the settlements system at one of the global hubs of finance.

Second, pointed out McRae, while having a system that works is important, a pretty good system that works is infinitely preferable to the pursuit of a perfect one that does not. Never let the perfect be the enemy of the good. At the TAURUS project, like almost any project anywhere, "scope creep" turned out to be its death knell. *Wouldn't it be great if this new system not only did everything we've already thought of and asked it to do, but also does this one other thing? And if it made perfect espressos while one is waiting for a trade to go through, that would be even more awesome,* and so on. Eventually, a project that was simple and well defined at the beginning becomes a Rube Goldberg device that is supposed to do all things for all people. And of course it ends up not being able to do even the simplest things that the designers set out to achieve in the first place.

I see this in companies all the time through one enterprise-wide system: SAP. SAP is the market leader in what are called enterprise resource planning (ERP) systems. ERP systems are supposed to do everything. They are giant databases that track resources, like cash, raw materials, or production capacity, and match those to payroll, invoices, orders, and so on. So an ERP system touches every part of a company—procurement, sales, HR, accounting, production, just about everything really—and integrates them digitally. It actually works pretty well for that, if you use it off the shelf.

The issue comes when, like TAURUS, people get really excited with their magical solution to *everything*: integrate every system, talk to the older mainframes in the basement, handle cloud computing, stitch together the patchwork systems that various departments have jerry-rigged and use. (Or replace them altogether! With something better!) And so the scope creep begins. *Let's have it talk to this existing system that we've been using for thirty years.* Or *It should include every feature of that off-the-shelf product that we bought twenty years ago and is no longer supported.* The list is endless.

I've worked with three global corporations in the past six months alone who have been trying to implement SAP for more than a decade. At one global beverage company—you've probably had one of their products today—after I spoke about keeping things simple, an engineer sidled up to me and spoke sotto voce. "We've spent more than a billion on it," he said. "And it still doesn't work." At another company with hundreds of thousands of employees working in some of the most remote areas of the planet, they told me a billion dollars was cheap. They had spent a billion and a half on SAP and it didn't work. I won't depress you with the third example. Trust me, it's bad. All three had one thing in common: despite those billions of dollars and thousands of people, it didn't work. And yet they keep throwing hundreds of millions a year more at the problem, doing things the same way and expecting different results.

But back to TAURUS, that perfect jewel of a settlements system, and those poor souls with the Sisyphean task to integrate seventeen different proposals for how the system should work. It was supposed to be all things to all people. They tried. They truly did.

For the last problem with TAURUS, I'm just going to quote a paragraph from McRae here:

> The Stock Exchange has not been listening to its customers. It has many different types of customer: the member firms, the companies whose shares it trades, the institutional investors, the personal investors. The members were worried about the costs of TAURUS, the companies were unhappy (and some had refused to help), the institutions were at best indifferent or at worst hostile, and any small investors who knew about it were disturbed about the additional charges they seemed likely to have to pay. It takes a particular arrogance to press on with something against this sort of resistance.

"A particular arrogance"—the arrogance of the expert. The arrogance of the professional. The arrogance of the bureaucrat. The arrogance of process over people, putting more value on the intricate descriptions of things that work rather than on the things themselves. The egotistical insistence that an elaborate plan they put their hearts and minds into trumped the more prudent idea that things might change, so maybe it'd be a good idea to put together a plan for that.

So TAURUS, born a beautiful idea, was canceled in 1993 after years of effort, thousands of people working long days and late nights, and some £75 million flushed down the toilet. The total cost impact to stakeholders is estimated at some £400 million.

That's a lot. But also a lot of wasted time and wasted lives. A bunch of really smart people dedicated years to creating something that became synonymous with technological disaster.

And as much as I wish I could tell you that TAURUS is one of the worst examples I can give you, it isn't. There are lots more. The National Health System project Connecting for Health, which was supposed to create electronic health records in the United Kingdom: nine years wasted, at a cost of £12 billion. The Expeditionary Combat Support System for the U.S. military: seven years wasted, at a cost of $1.1 billion. The California Department of Motor Vehicles spent tens of millions of dollars starting in 1987 building a system that by 1990 was worse than the system it was supposed to replace—and yet they could not bring themselves to call it quits until 1994. The *San Francisco Chronicle* described it as "an unworkable system that could not be fixed without the expenditure of millions more."

Our machines became faster and more capable, but we humans had nothing to show for it—that was the context that my father was working in back in the early 1990s. If you want the full story of what took place, read *Scrum: The Art of Doing Twice the Work in Half the Time*. But in brief, he came up with a new way of working. His critical insight was that these kinds of failures weren't due to the people involved. The managers and engineers and designers on those massive projects that failed weren't bad people. They weren't stupid. They didn't set out to fail. They set out with grand dreams and goals of making a difference, of changing how the world did things.

It wasn't the people who failed, it was the system. It was the way they were working, how they thought about what had to happen when they went to meetings to discuss and plan their efforts. To them, it was just the way things were done. To work any other way would be like a fish questioning the species's deep commitment to water.

A Survival Guide

People whose jobs are in danger from automation really aren't any different from corporations whose reason for existence is under constant threat. Whether you are making personal choices about your work, planning the strategic goals for a large multinational, or deciding how a culture will adapt to a new set of circumstances with a vastly different set of axioms, the ability to rapidly adapt will determine your success. As my father and I wrote in our last book: *change or die*.

In this book, though, I want to give you a few more tools. I'm going to take you around the globe and from outer space to call centers, from radical new technologies to a restaurant. The trends can seem scary, but I truly believe we can learn to embrace the change to make us more resilient and less afraid, to make us capable of more, to not bemoan what we can no longer do, to act with global purpose rather than be trapped by the forces around us.

Because the real trick is that Scrum itself does nothing. All it does is unleash the greatness that lives within all of us. That greatness is there. It can be hidden or beaten down, but it can never be truly lost. It's what we humans are. One day we think the world works one way; the next we find out it doesn't, in fact, work that way. In a moment, we can realize we've been looking at the world through a narrow lens, that there is a universe of possibilities we never thought of, and now, suddenly, we can reshape how the world works . . . and really we always could.

THE TAKEAWAY

Scrum is the art of changing the possible. You can adapt to this world of accelerating change and see what you, your organization, your peers, and your people are truly capable of. Whether you are making personal choices about your work or planning the strategic goals for a large multinational, the ability to rapidly adapt will determine your fate.

Failure is inevitable and invaluable. It doesn't matter who was responsible for a company's success or failure, or how the money was spent, or what went wrong. The best organizations learn from their mistakes and successes and then systematically use those lessons to get better.

Perfection is overrated. A pretty good system that works is infinitely preferable to the pursuit of a perfect one that does not.

BACKLOG

- Go through each of the four Agile values and assess how Agile you and your organization are. Remember, "there is value in the items on the right, but we value the items on the left more."

    - Individuals and interactions over processes and tools

    - Working software (product or service) over comprehensive documentation

    - Customer collaboration over contract negotiation

    - Responding to change over following a plan

    - Examine your organization's response to failure. Is it a valuable learning opportunity or a time to point fingers?

- Assess your and your organization's ability to adapt and innovate. How easily can you keep pace with changing demands, wants, and requirements? Are you a disruptor, or are you waiting to be made irrelevant? What is helping or hurting your ability to react to change?

CHAPTER 2

Making It Cheap to Change Your Mind

My colleague Joe Justice has a simple refrain: "Scrum is about reducing the cost of changing your mind." Joe works mainly with companies producing hard goods: cars, rockets, medical devices, personal protection equipment for firefighters, that kind of thing. You know, stuff.

The problems he runs into aren't unique to the "stuff" industry—your understanding of what the product should be, what the features are, what you need to do to meet high standards, how you deliver it at a reasonable cost and at a speed driven by the needs of your customers and the actions of your competitors. It is the same no matter what business you are in.

In *The Scrum Fieldbook*, I'm going to lay out the patterns and practices that allow us to solve those problems faster than you think possible. But before I dive into that, I want to give you a brief overview of the basics of Scrum.

How Scrum Works

So here's how Scrum works.

First, you need to understand that there are three, and only three, roles in Scrum: the Product Owner, the Scrum Master, and the Team Member. There's no business analyst, there's no tech lead, there's no senior Scrum Master—only those three roles. They make up a Scrum Team that is able to independently deliver value. The Team is the smallest organizational unit in Scrum. These Teams rapidly deliver value to customers in short cycles called Sprints.

The Product Owner, or PO, owns the "what." What the Team is going to build or create or service to deliver or process to write or put out. The PO takes input from customers, stakeholders, the Team itself, and whoever is going to get value from whatever the Team is doing. It could be rural farmers in Uganda struggling with crop disease, or engineers building an autonomous car, or filmgoers going to see a newly released movie. The PO has to take all of that input, some of which may be contradictory, and create a vision of what the Team will do. Then—and this is often the hard part—after getting all those ideas, the Product Owner has to rank them in order from the most valuable to the least. There are no top priorities in Scrum—there is only one priority at a time. This is often hard to settle on. But that's the way Scrum works.

So the PO prioritizes all the stuff that has to be done, from the most valuable to the least valuable, creating what is called the Product Backlog. This Product Backlog is a potentially infinite list of all the possible things that could be tackled by this Team. It is also a living document, constantly changing, based on feedback from customers, changing market conditions, insights, management, whatever. It is designed to make change easy.

Then the Product Owner presents that backlog to the Team in an event called Sprint Planning. At this event, the Team looks at the Product Backlog and decides what to tackle and how much they think they can get done during the next Sprint. Note that the Team decides, not the PO or management. They pull the top items of the Product Backlog into what is called the Sprint Backlog. While the Product Backlog is infinitely fungible, the Sprint Backlog is fixed. You want the Team to focus on those items and only those items for the next Sprint.

Then they are off to the races. They execute a Sprint of one to four weeks—whatever rhythm works best for the Team. Most companies do two-week Sprints these days, but I always recommend one-week Sprints to my clients. The reason for that is the Scrum process has built-in feedback loops. I like those loops to be short so that we can learn really quickly. This is especially critical to Teams that work in areas like sales, customer support, or finance, where responsiveness is crucial.

The next event is the Daily Scrum, often called the Standup. This event lasts only fifteen minutes. In it the Team shares what they have been doing to work toward the goal of that Sprint, what they will be doing in the next twenty-four hours, and anything that they see that might get in the way of the Team meeting their goal. The Daily Scrum is not a status meeting. It's like a football huddle. A mini re-planning session. The Team has learned things as they are doing the work, and this is a chance to share that learning from the previous day. It's like a group of people heading out on a road trip: they plan the route to their destination, get on the road, and then each day at breakfast they check the map, the weather, whose turn it is to drive, then get back out on the road. After fifteen minutes, the Daily Scrum is over.

Now enters the Scrum Master. That's a weird job title, isn't it? I actually lobbied my father, the co-creator of Scrum, to change it to something else, like "coach." He told me it was already too baked into the culture. Too late. Ah, well. Now, the Scrum Master role is a new thing in most companies. Their entire job is to help the Teams go faster. *Speed* is the altar they worship at.

Why would you pay someone to do this? Well, if they can make your Team produce value twice as quickly, they have more than paid for themselves. It is always better to make your Teams go faster than to hire more people or Teams. So the Scrum Master helps a Team build speed (what Scrum measures as Velocity), and the Product Owner is responsible for turning that speed into value. There's nothing quite as sad as a really excellent group of people making things that no one wants, really quickly. Remember Nokia Mobile? They had some good Scrum Teams there making phones incredibly fast—phones, of course, that no one wanted once they'd seen an iPhone. They went from being the dominant player in the mobile market to having a market value of zero in only a few short years.

So the Scrum Master is like the coach of a sports team. They help the Teams with the Scrum process and try to get things out of their way that are slowing them down. That is their sole job. Every day.

As the Team is working away on the Sprint Backlog, sometime during the Sprint they need to sit down with the Product Owner during what is called Backlog Refinement. This is where Scrum lives or dies, in my opinion. It's in this event that the Product Owner brings in all their great ideas for future Sprints and works with the Team to make those ideas ready to execute. They decide precisely what a certain item entails, and—most important—what criteria will be used to judge whether that item is done or not.

Let's take something that I do a lot: writing a blog post. Now, it would be easy for me to say, *Hey, I've written it, it's done.* But is it really? It needs to be edited. It needs to be proofread. It needs to have a picture. It needs to be put on the website. And someone has to push "publish." You don't get any value from me writing a blog post until all of those things happen. It's important to make sure all the work is captured, not just your little piece.

These criteria can be simple, like a picture on a page, or they can be complex, like work that must meet FDA regulatory requirements on human safety before it can be done because the Team's project is implantable medical devices. The importance of ready work cannot be overstated—it will double a Team's productivity. The reason is pretty simple. If the work to be done isn't clear, and if the quality standards are not known, the Team will spend an inordinate amount of time trying to figure out what the work actually is, and often will find out they can't start working on it because that piece of work is dependent on another piece of work that another Team is working on.

At the end of the Sprint, the Team and the Product Owner hold a Sprint Review. This is when they show their stakeholders and customers what they have finished, what they have done. And by done, I mean *done*—not almost done, not kind of done, not something someone worked really hard on but didn't finish and shouldn't that work be praised. Done. And the Team and the Product Owner will get feedback from whoever is in the room: *We like this. We don't like that. What about this? Now that we've seen this, what we really want next is* . . . The Product Owner uses this feedback to reprioritize the Product Backlog, as they now have concrete data from real customers on what the customers actually want, not what they say they want.

There's an old rule of thumb in software, called Humphrey's law: basically, people don't know what they want until they see what they don't want. You can get them to write down their wishes in documents thousands of pages long, but until they actually see something that works, they don't really know what they want. And out of the Sprint Review comes a potentially releasable piece of work. It might be too small to put into service, or maybe it isn't valuable until a lot more things are done, but that small piece, that bit, is completely and totally done. Never needs to be touched again.

The final output of the Sprint Review is a measure of how much stuff the Team got done during that Sprint. How fast they are in producing value. We call this the Team's Velocity. This is the key metric in Scrum. We want to know how fast Teams are and whether we can help them go faster, to accelerate.

When you look at history, it's amazing how often small events that seem almost inconsequential at the time turn out to be the pivot upon which the future turned. It's the whole "for want of a nail, the kingdom was lost" kind of thing. The first Sprint Review was one of those.

The first Scrum Team was working on something technically complex, so they couldn't ask a regular customer to come in and look at what they were doing. My father recruited some technical experts in and around the Massachusetts Institute of Technology to take a look. They were brutal. The experts questioned the Team's skills, pointed out fundamental flaws, mistaken assumptions, and so on. The Team was devastated. I've been told it was not an easy day, and by the time they were done, the Team just wanted to put their heads down on the table and give up. They looked at Jeff and told him there was no way they could go through that again. It would break them.

"Okay," said my father. "You have a choice right now. You can be just another software development team, or you can be a great software development team. I can't make you do it. You get to pick."

That moment, that decision by those seven people changed the world. It is why you are reading this book and why millions of people around the world now work in a better way. There aren't many times in history when you can say that moment, this day, those people, that is what did it. This was the moment Scrum was born.

"Okay," they said. "One more time."

And the rest is history.

The last event in Scrum is the Sprint Retrospective. This is the examination of how the Team is working together. The Sprint Review is about what was built or what service was provided. The Sprint Retrospective is about how it was done. The Product Owner, the Scrum Master, and the Team sit down and try to figure out what went well, what could have gone better, and what the Team wants to change in how they work to make things better and faster next Sprint. Then the next Sprint begins. Rinse and repeat.

So that's it, that's Scrum. I'm going to spend the rest of this book on how this simple framework has changed the world, has allowed organizations to adapt and take advantage of the ever-accelerating pace of change, and might just save your company, your career, and maybe even your life.

The Real World Always Changes

I'm going to give you two quick examples of how Scrum has worked in real situations, to answer the question I am often asked: "Sure, that sounds great, but what about in the real world?" I'll leave aside for the moment the odd assumption baked into that question that there is a "real world." Let me first take you to the often snow-covered streets of Minneapolis, Minnesota, and a guy named Tom Auld. Tom flips houses. And he does it using Scrum.

It starts out in a normal enough fashion: Tom identifies a house to flip, usually in the $80,000–$100,000 range. Then he puts together his Team. Now, his Team is made up of contractors—usually a couple of general contractors, an electrician, a plumber, and a carpenter. These are all people who can work for whomever they choose, but they choose to work with Tom.

Tom and the Team walk through the house, talking about what will need to be done to make the house sellable. That is, they build a backlog. They put the backlog up on a wall in the house in three columns with Post-its: "To Do," "Doing," and "Done" (Scrum uses Post-it notes by the pallet—Super Sticky FTW), and the Team discusses what each item entails (be it tearing down a wall or refinishing a floor) and agrees on what it means for each of those Post-it notes to be moved from the "To Do" column of the backlog to the "Done" column. When they all agree the work is clear and how much effort they think it will take, they start to work.

They break up their work into six Sprints, each one week long. Usually the first is demolition. They then spend, on average, two Sprints on electrical and plumbing and structural work, a couple more on specific improvements, and then a final Sprint on finishing touches. Each week they get together, plan the work they are going to do for that Sprint, agree on the definition of *done* for each of those tasks, and get to work. Every day the whole Team looks at the backlog and then they decide as a Team how they are going to attack the work in order to get that week's goal to done. Sure, there are specialties, but they know that they succeed or fail as a Team. At the end of the week, Tom shows up and they conduct a Sprint Review by walking through the house together, agreeing on what work is done, what isn't, and how this Sprint's work will affect the backlog for the coming Sprints. Maybe they tore down a wall and, as is not uncommon when fixing up houses, discovered that what they thought would be easy would be difficult—maybe a raccoon family has set up shop in the walls, or the wiring isn't up to code, whatever. And as they work through what is done, Tom pays them for their work that week. Often in contracting, builders aren't paid until the entire project is done, and even then clients are often slow to pay, but Tom insists on paying for incremental value delivered.

That Sprint Review, looking at the actual work accomplished, also impacts what they will be able to accomplish in the rest of the project. Tom has a budget, and if things look like they will be more expensive than they thought, the Team may decide to reduce scope. Maybe that new wainscoting in the dining room, which would be nice to have, simply won't be able to be done. The Team is able to change their work in real time based on what is actually happening, rather than blindly following a plan with the potential of ballooning costs.

Every week after the Sprint Review they sit down and talk about how they are working together. How can the electrician and the carpenter work better together in the next week? Is there a better way to handle the inevitable dependencies that crop up in any work? Dependencies are when you have to wait for someone or something before you can keep going. Things like, *Oh, we have to wait for a part from Home Depot*, or *He has to finish his work before I can begin mine*. They take what they learn each week to change what they are going to do, reacting to the conditions on the ground, and how they are going to go about it, reacting to the flow of work in this particular project. While the houses are, in general, similar, in any specific house the work is always a bit different each time.

Tom's role, as the Product Owner, has a number of responsibilities. He picks the most profitable house to flip. He prioritizes the renovations by business value: maybe they could either redo the bathroom or blow out the kitchen, but he decides which one has more value. Each day, at the end of the workday, Tom looks at the work, and only he can move something to done. As a result, he can iteratively react to increase revenue. His Team appreciates clarity, the lack of rework, and getting paid regularly and on time. They are in demand, but they choose most often to work with Tom, not because of the work they are doing but because of how they organize the work.

Let me stress the importance of reducing rework. Sometimes in house remodeling there are time and materials that are extremely expensive, like doing intricate restoration of antique carpentry. That requires highly skilled craftspeople and usually really costly wood. But by doing a bit of the work—say, just a portion of some fancy crown molding—and then showing the customer, they have invested only a small amount of time and money. If the customer then says, *You know, I know I insisted on oak, but now that I see it, I want mahogany,* it becomes less of a big deal than if a whole floor was done one way and then the customer insists upon a change. An incremental approach reduces the cost of changing your mind. You can respond to the conditions of work—that family of raccoons—and rapid customer feedback.

We know the work is going to change. We know the customer will change their mind once they see something (remember Humphrey's law). Instead of fighting those inevitable changes, Scrum embraces them. With large projects, sometimes whole organizations are set up to resist change. They have change requests and Change Control Boards charged with limiting change. And because we know things will always change, basically what they are doing is paying people to *make sure* the customer doesn't get what they want.

Go Big or Go Home

Let me give you another example—it's on a bigger scale, but the process is exactly the same. Let's take 3M. 3M makes everything from Post-it notes to respirators to the tape for lane marking to automotive window film to dental equipment to healthcare software. Their revenue was over $30 billion in 2017. They operate globally. You have almost certainly used a 3M product today.

In March 2017, I held a few training classes in Saint Paul for people from various 3M divisions. One guy stood out in the class, a manager named Mark Anderson. He couldn't tell me what he was doing exactly but asked if Scrum had ever been used in mergers and acquisitions. I told him quite honestly that I wasn't aware of it ever being used that way, but I couldn't see why it couldn't be done.

A few weeks later, I came across this press release:

> 3M (NYSE: MMM) today announced that it has entered into a definitive agreement to acquire Scott Safety from Johnson Controls for a total enterprise value of $2.0 billion. Scott Safety is a premier manufacturer of innovative products, including self-contained breathing apparatus (SCBA) systems, gas and flame detection instruments, and other safety devices that complement 3M's personal safety portfolio.

"Two billion dollars is a lot of money," I told Mark when I saw him again. He said it was the second-largest acquisition in the history of 3M, which started more than a hundred years ago, and he had just been put in charge of integration. "No pressure," I said with a smile. Then he told me he was going to try doing it with Scrum, and that if he could, he'd let me know afterward how it went.

If you've never done it, integrating an acquisition is hard, let alone one of that size. There are operational issues, sales, salaries and HR, processes, marketing, finance, research and development. In my experience, often the trickiest part is culture—

bringing an acquisition with a corporate culture of its own into the culture of the new mothership. This can be especially challenging when both groups have strong cultures of their own. 3M has a remarkable engineering culture with a generations-long history. People's lives depend on their products working right the first time and every time. Scott Safety had a similar ethos. Respiratory protection, thermal sensors, and other devices for firefighters must work correctly the first time and every time.

Mark called me up near the end of 2017 to tell me that not only had they done it, but it would have been a different story if they had done it in a traditional way. The traditional way of project management is known to Scrum people as "waterfall." In waterfall, people try to map out the whole project before even starting. They gather all the possible requirements that are going to be needed—at times these run into the thousands. I've seen requirements documents that stand a few feet high when you print them out. Everyone signs off in the mutually agreed-upon delusion that they've actually read them all, and then the project management team divides the work into phases. *First we'll do this part,* they say, *and that will take two weeks.* They draw a bar at the top of what is called a Gantt chart. *Then we'll do this next phase; that will take two months.* And they'll draw a bar on the graph below and to the right of the first one. And so on, and so on. Like a beautiful waterfall. This color-coded chart can go on for months, years even—I've seen ones feet high and meters long. They truly can be works of art. Gorgeous. And they are always wrong. Always. Because nothing goes according to plan. Ever. Something always happens. So those bars get moved. Things will not be delivered on time. Now the project is late. So the chart is wrong. But the chart *can't* be wrong. So they hire people to make the chart look like reality as reality changes. It's a basic human flaw: *If I just can think hard enough about this, I can remove all error.* It's the *illusion* of control.

"Scrum allowed us to change strategy, learn as we were doing, and seize opportunities late in the process," said Mark. The key, he said, was to react and respond quickly to the inevitable changes that arose, both risks and opportunities.

So how did they do it? Well, the first thing they did was put together a backlog of what they needed to accomplish. Next, what areas of expertise did they need to execute on that? So they put together a cross-functional Team of Product Owners who had those skills: finance, research and development, sales, marketing, HR. These were the groups that would have to coordinate all the things that would have to be integrated so that Scott Safety would become part of 3M.

Each of those Product Owners had a Team. Or a Team of Teams. And while Mark says the level of Scrum was imperfect, and that really only IT and R&D did it all the way down, that top level of coordination was critical. The most important thing? Those Product Owners were continually getting together to coordinate efforts, share knowledge, ask each other for help, and reprioritize the backlog as new information became available. For example, if finance needed data on salaries, that would go onto the Product Backlog for the whole integration and each Team would know what they needed to deliver to get that piece of the work done.

Six months. That was all they had: six months. So everyone laid out their high-level goals and headlines, and then they would pull their weekly backlogs from a coordinated high-level backlog for the entire effort.

They worked in one-week Sprints. Every Wednesday they would review the backlog, prioritize the work for the coming week, estimate the effort for each of the items they thought they could get done that Sprint, and begin work. They weren't doing Scrum exactly the way I laid it out: they were meeting three times a week for fifteen minutes for their Daily Scrum, not every day. So they would meet on Friday and check in, then on Monday. Then each Wednesday, before planning the next week, they would examine how much they actually got done, not what they said they would.

Mark says the impact was dramatic. First of all the visibility: the state of the effort was obvious and clear at all times. There was no doubt where things stood, because a visible board broadcast the information constantly. He also says that by simply focusing on getting faster, rather than just hoping they would get done, they did get faster.

They also had problems, he said. They didn't do Retrospectives as rigorously as they could have, and they think they could have improved even more if they had. But the high level of visibility was able to reveal where slowdowns were occurring.

The result? On the first day, all the managers were in place and every employee had a place to report. Finance was ready to go immediately—no troubles with different and muddled forecasting, everything was tracked and visible. There was a global kick-off, the right signage was in place, the HR policies were clear. The incredibly complicated interlocking parts of a massive integration fit together precisely. 3M prides itself as constantly innovating, not just its products but the way it operates. As far as I know, this was the first time Scrum had ever been used to complete a multibillion-dollar corporate merger. And it worked.

One thing that Mark added stuck with me. As they were working through the integration, late in the game they identified three separate market opportunities that they could seize and which would immediately have a financial impact—if they acted quickly. So they did. They threw away some of their plan and changed what they were doing to take advantage of these new things they had learned.

3M is a company that prides itself on collaboration. I've heard the company has used Scrum in all sorts of ways because Agile thinking fits with its culture. And as some at 3M will tell you, Scrum fosters Agile thinking.

Change Always Changes

Whether you are flipping a house or integrating a multibillion-dollar acquisition, the power of Scrum is making change cheap. We know there will be change. The only question is, do you fight that change or harness it?

The Standish Group reports that in any project, 67 percent of requirements change during development. Why? Well, people learn as they do. As we build something, we learn that some things that seemed really important aren't. We learn that while the customer said one thing, and even signed that stack of requirements, they really didn't know, or the market changes, or the world changes.

You didn't start out your career with the goal of not delivering what people want. No one does. We all want to create great stuff, fantastic services, awesome products, amazing new things. But the system we build to protect our educated but ultimately false vision of the future—the system that we set up to protect our egos and reputations—has delivered us a world where nothing gets done. We spin our wheels trying, but we just can't get things out the door. We ossify our organizations so it becomes impossible to do so. We have documents and studies and charts and panels set up to try to insist we were right.

But we're not. We never are. We will always have to change our minds as we learn more about ourselves, our capabilities, our customers, our world.

The whole point is to make that change fast, cheap, and fun. If it isn't, you ain't doing it right.

THE TAKEAWAY

Remember Humphrey's law. You can't fight Humphrey's law. But you can harness it. If people don't know what they want until they see what they don't want, get your feedback fast, then adjust your course quickly.

Lies and "waterfalls." Reduce risk and increase the chances of success—those are the promises of traditional project management or "waterfall" systems. The problem is they don't work. Planning every detail out in advance ignores the inevitable fact that something unexpected will always happen. Always. When was the last time you saw a Gantt chart that was right?

The 3-5-3 of Scrum. There are just three roles in Scrum: Product Owner, Scrum Master, and Team Member. There are five events: Sprint Planning, the Sprint, the Daily Scrum, the Sprint Review, and the Sprint Retrospective. And there are three artifacts: the Product Backlog, the Sprint Backlog, and the Increment of product the Team delivers each Sprint. It's not complicated. It does require discipline, though.

BACKLOG

- Start incorporating the 3-5-3 of Scrum at your workplace.
- Who will prioritize?
- Who will coach?
- Who will do the work?
- Build a Product Backlog.
- Plan your first Sprint.
- *Go!*
- Meet daily to coordinate and re-plan.
- Have something completely done at the end of the Sprint.
- Reflect on what went well and what could have gone better, and decide how you will do better next time.
- Rinse and repeat.

CHAPTER 3

Why We Can't Decide

You've got a problem—you just discovered it.

It could be anything. You're building something and realize the design really does need to be changed. You stumble across something you hadn't anticipated when you planned the work, and you need to decide what to do. *Should I do that really urgent thing now, or should I wait and work on the hugely important thing that will be incredibly valuable later?*

It's like Dwight D. Eisenhower's famous decision quadrant, where he ranked things by importance and urgency:

	Urgent	Not Urgent
Important	**Quadrant 1** Important and urgent tasks. (Crises, deadlines, problems)	**Quadrant 2** Important but not urgent tasks. (Relationships, planning, recreation)
Not Important	**Quadrant 3** Urgent but not important tasks. (Interruptions, meetings, activities)	**Quadrant 4** Not important and not urgent tasks. (Time wasters, pleasure)

So now you're stuck, and you have to decide which of those quadrants your fresh, new, hairy problem fits in.

Whom do you need to check with? Do you have to wait for a committee to meet? Is everyone's calendar so full there is no way you can get a decision today—maybe tomorrow, probably the day after? And what is the cost of that delay?

Decision Latency

Jim Johnson, the founder and chairman of the Standish Group, started to get interested in this question a few years ago. The Standish Group does primary research on how projects are run globally through interviews, focus groups, and surveys. They've been doing this since 1985. We're talking tens of thousands of projects. Regularly they publish the CHAOS Report, with all sorts of fascinating data about what makes projects succeed or fail.

The chart that has been driving the adoption of Agile globally is this one:

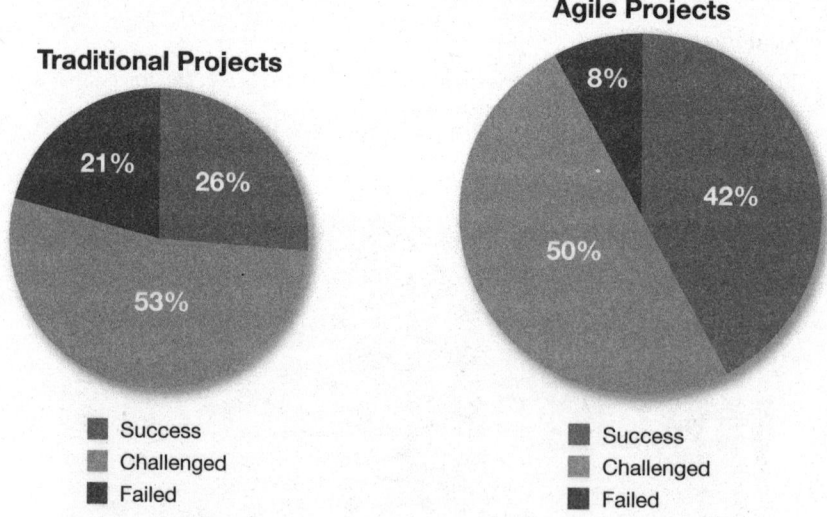

On average Agile projects have a 42% success rate compared to 26% for traditional projects.

Agile projects, and Scrum is the way most of those are done, are less than half as likely to fail as traditional projects, and succeed far more often. That's the math.

But let's be clear: not every Agile project ends well. Scrum Inc. and Jim have been looking into why 50 percent of Agile projects are still challenged, late, over budget, or leave customers unhappy.

What is the root cause of project failure? What is it about Scrum projects that makes them so much more likely to succeed? It came to Jim one day while he was interviewing the head of the Massachusetts state purchasing office years ago.

"He told me this story," says Jim. "Previously he had worked at Boston City Hall. And he talked about this situation where they had to get a decision from the deputy mayor to move ahead with this project. They had sixty contractors waiting for that decision. Sixty people couldn't move for six weeks. It took that long to make a decision."

Jim was astounded. This had to be an aberration. So he started adding the question "How fast do you make decisions?" to his research. And when he looked at the projects that had problems, he realized that it wasn't an aberration, it was commonplace. In projects that failed, people simply weren't making decisions. What he found really weird was that most of the time the decisions involved weren't extraordinarily complex or difficult. They were usually common, everyday decisions. But they simply weren't being *made*!

He kept running into this over and over and over again as he started asking the question, so he started to benchmark it—to actually measure how long it took people to make a decision about a project once they knew a decision had to be made. Because in any project you have to make a lot of decisions.

"It turns out," says Jim, "the data shows you have to make a decision for about every thousand dollars you spend on a project.

So for a million-dollar project, you're going to have to make about a thousand decisions." That adds up quick. And the longer those decisions take, the more expensive it will be due to that wonderful corollary to Einstein's Theory of General Relativity: not only are time and space the same thing, but so are time and money. So Jim came up with a metric that measures how long it takes from the time it is clear a decision has to be made to when the decision is made. He calls it "decision latency." He then compared that to the likelihood of project success. He looked at hundreds of projects globally. The results? It's worse than you think.

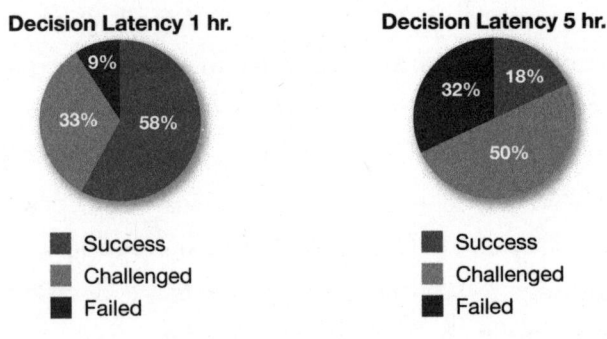

Standish Group 2013–2017

The charts show the end result of many hundreds of projects. For projects where decisions could be made quickly, in under an hour, 58 percent of them succeed (they are on time and on budget). If it takes you more than five hours to make a decision, your odds of success plummet: only 18 percent of those projects work. Five hours. That is not a lot of time.

It took Jim a year to decide to release his research, because it was so shocking. So he did presentations at business schools and workshops before publishing.

"The response has been really interesting," Jim reflected. "At first they say, 'No, that can't be true. That can't be the root cause.'

And then they think about it for a while. And they come around and say, 'You actually might be on to something.'"

Here's the real kicker: most of those decisions are trivial and easy. But if you have a rigid, hierarchical process where decisions have to go up the chain to be approved and then flow back down, that journey takes a long time.

At a large global automotive company we've worked with, they use a common Japanese approval system called a *ringi*. The aim is to create consensus among the management as to what a decision should be. When someone proposes something, it gets circulated around to everyone in the decision-making chain; once everyone agrees with it and senior leadership has signed off, the decision is made. The idea is that you must work quietly in the background to build consensus, to make the ground fertile for a proposal. The Japanese call this *nemawashi*—literally, "going around the roots," in the sense of digging around the roots of a tree as you prepare to transplant it.

Let me tell you one kind of depressing story about how it works. Let's say you are working at an automotive factory here in America and you want to spend money on something, say a new piece of equipment for the plant. Even though money has already been allocated for that new equipment in the annual budget, you have to submit a *ringi*—on paper. You have to write a detailed and persuasive business case for why you want to spend the money. You also have to include all the accounting data: how much money you are going to spend, where it comes from, whom it goes to. Again, on paper. Then there's the environmental review: how much electricity the machine will use, what emissions impact it might have. All of this gets written down on paper too. That stack of paper is the *ringi*.

Then it has to be approved. First it goes to the central planning group. As told to me by one of the engineers, "They have to review it, check it for a bunch of things we don't even understand." This central planning group then either kicks it back for changes or approves it.

Once it's approved, then it has to be signed—by hand, remember, since it's all on paper. First it needs to be signed by the manager of the person who requested it. Then by a senior manager. Then the group manager. Then the general manager. Probably the vice president. Oh, and then the manager, senior manager, group manager, general manager, and VP of the central planning group have to sign it as well. Since we're working in a manufacturing facility, we probably have to get the safety general manager to sign off too.

We're not done yet. Next that packet of papers with all those signatures has to go through the same approval chain in finance. If it has any impact on IT, the general manager and VP of information systems have to have those pages on their desk as well. And if the decision is big enough, the *ringi* packet might have to go to headquarters as well and go through a duplicate approval tree there.

The engineer I spoke with has only had to do a small one, for something that cost in the middle six figures. It required about thirty-five separate signatures, in pen, on the same piece of paper (and that wasn't extreme; sometimes fifty people have to sign). That took four to five months, and it can take longer—a lot longer. What they've done now is create a pre-*ringi ringi* so that they can get some money (money that has already been budgeted for this, mind you) to start vehicle development.

One group has been tasked with at least automating the whole thing. They're doing it, naturally, with Scrum. Their goal? Get rid of the paper. Moving paper around through numerous feedback loops is, shall we say, painfully slow. They're also going to automate some of the checks that the central planning group does.

This will have two benefits. First off, it will make the process *visible*. Right now no one knows whose desk those papers are sitting on, so no one can tell where it is in the process. Is it almost done? Halfway? Is it being held up by someone for some reason we just don't know? Second, as things stand now, if you want to copy a *ringi* from a few years ago, because you are asking for the same thing it did, you have to find the person who requested it, hope they've kept a paper copy (which may or may not be the case), and then copy it from there. By digitizing it, they'll at least be able to look back at a *ringi* that has been approved and copy it.

Because of all these layers, all these chains of approval, frequently the wrong person ends up making a given decision. There are different types of decisions. Some technical, some business, some involving personnel. And while some of those decisions are important, some aren't. And different decisions should be made by different types of people. You want the people who know the most to make the call in a given situation.

"Scrum is so neat because you can force decision down to the Team level," Jim says. "In Scrum you really have only two decision-makers, the Product Owner and the Team. And so stakeholders or executives have fewer decisions to make."

That's the key. Only the people who actually have the most knowledge and understand the most about it should make the decision. And that's how you do it fast. If it is taking more than five hours to make a decision, it is an almost sure sign that you had to send it up a chain for approval.

One hour. That's the goal. That's how fast decisions need to be made. Waiting for the committee to decide is entering into a suicide pact with destiny. So how do we drive that decision-making time down?

Measure Your Meetings

So, you have a decision to make. So you decide to have a meeting. Say there are twenty people in the meeting, and it takes an hour to come to a decision. Ask yourself: how much did that decision cost? Just for the time alone. The amount of money spent on that hour. Now think about all the pointless meetings you are in every week.

A friend of mine used to work at an Ivy League university. He told me sometimes he would walk into a meeting without even knowing why he was there. Even if he did, the meetings would just go on and on. We walked through the math as an exercise. Each meeting, we figured, cost about a thousand bucks. He went to, at a minimum, ten to fifteen of those a week. That adds up.

The real problem, though, is even worse: decisions made in meetings are very likely to be reversed. According to the Standish data, more than 40 percent of decisions made in meetings are overturned. Let's say that a decision is made in one meeting. And let's say it's a week until the next meeting. During that week the first decision begins to be implemented. Then at the next meeting everyone changes their mind and a new decision is made. So not only do you have the waste of a week of time, but now you have to go undo all the work that was just done. It's like digging holes and filling them back in again. Work with no purpose.

There are two reasons this happens, according to the Standish Group's research: the people who were in the meeting, and the people who weren't. The decision the people who are actually in the room come to is often made by the loudest person in that room. They bulldoze everyone else to get the decision they want. Then after the meeting is over, people go back to their offices and say, *Huh—I don't really agree with that decision, now that I come to think of it. I'll bring that up at the meeting next week.*

And then there are those people who weren't in the room. Maybe they should have been. They certainly feel they should have been anyway. Why weren't they consulted? Well, they will certainly show up at the next meeting to be *heard*.

A project fails a day at a time, says Jim Johnson. Each day of delay makes it more likely to fail. One day at time: a slow march to disaster.

Deciding Which Decisions to Make

Scrum is set up to reveal the issues that are slowing you down. It exposes them. Shoves them into the light. Of course, when problems keep coming up Sprint after Sprint, and the Team rightly expects them to be addressed, some people start saying the problem is Scrum rather than the problem itself. But the problem was always there.

The problem with problems is that there are different kinds of problems. And the solutions to these problems lie not in the heads of the management in the head office; rather, they lie with those who have direct contact with customers—out in the "nodes," if you will. Often as people move up the executive ranks they become more distant from what is actually happening on the front lines while at the same time more convinced they have the best insight into solutions.

One radical example of pushing decisions out is Mirai Industry Company. They make electrical installation equipment—switch boxes, cable, tubes, stuff like that. Unlike most Japanese companies, they don't do the whole *ringi* bit. The founder and longtime CEO until his death in 2014 was Akio Yamada. Yamada thought the whole *ringi* thing was ridiculous and banned it. *Do your job as you think best,* he told his employees. *Let the people closest to the work do it.* "I'm a fool," Yamada wrote in his book *The Happiest Company to Work For.* "So how can I judge?" Within his own company, he often learned of new sales offices opening up around Japan by seeing someone's new business card. Employees would decide on their own to create a new office; they would rent a space in a building and hire and develop new employees. If he didn't allow people to make their own decisions that way, he wrote, people would have to spend enormous amounts of energy convincing their boss to do something the boss simply didn't understand.

However, in most companies, the bosses insist that they be educated on the whole thing and make the final decision. This leads to decisions being made by the people who know the least about the situation. Because they fear they don't have enough information, they ask for more. That delays the system. And then they become afraid they might make a mistake, so they call a committee meeting to spread the ownership of the decision around.

I know a committee at a large bank that has more than forty people on it. It's the risk committee, and any proposal for just about anything has to be approved by this committee. They debate for hours on these endless, soul-killing conference calls. By the time a decision is actually made, it's no longer clear whose idea it was and what problem they were trying to solve in the first place. And no individual can be held accountable if it turns out to be a bad idea. This committee was set up to protect the bank, which had made some sloppy decisions and was fined tens of millions of dollars by the government as a result. They really didn't want that to happen again. So they put all these really important people on this committee, telling the regulators, *Look, our senior leadership is making sure we don't do those sorts of things again.* Now, however, the risk committee doesn't just stop bad decisions; it stops any decision at all. It can take months. And when a decision is at long last made by these dozens of people, so much political capital has been invested in that decision it can never be, just maybe, the wrong decision. That would be impossible with that much executive intellectual throw weight applied to the issue. No, it has to be those pesky people who actually do things who failed to implement the decision that was made. This kind of risk committee is incredibly common in the financial sector, sadly.

The problem is that control functions tend to metastasize. What at first was a very narrowly defined remit can quickly grow far beyond its original intent. These aren't bad people. But they have created a system for controlling decisions, for getting buy-in, that doesn't merely slow things down, it almost ensures that the wrong decision will be made, because by the time they do make a decision, almost certainly the moment has passed. It's already been resolved one way or another in the intervening days or weeks. If you choose not to decide, you still have made a choice.

It Can't Work Here

There's a common refrain I hear from Scrum skeptics: *It can't work here. What we do is too complex. Too unpredictable. Too difficult for a system that gives autonomy to teams.* For some reason I can't quite fathom why they think traditional project management actually can handle their special snowflake of a project, but they believe it fervently. Or they say that it may be fine for software, but in their super-complex domain that is so much more difficult than software it just can't apply.

I teach classes open to the public fairly often. And what is incredible is just the sheer range of people who come. They range from bankers, manufacturers, publishers, and those who make biopharmaceuticals to researchers, service providers, educators, and nonprofit workers. The students almost always represent an amazing diversity of industries, expertise, and roles.

But if you are one of those skeptics, I want to share with you the experience of one person who has implemented Scrum in a domain that is most probably higher-stakes and faster-moving, with far less room for error, than what you are trying to accomplish. Probably.

U.S. Navy Commander Jon Haase called me up a couple of years ago. He had recently taken command of an alphabet soup of a unit, EODMU2 (Explosive Ordnance Disposal Mobile Unit 2), and he wanted to implement Scrum in his unit. He wanted to go faster, with higher quality, in one of the most demanding environments on the planet.

Explosive Ordnance Disposal is the smallest of the U.S. Special Forces, a couple thousand people. But they have to be able to deploy with any of the other units anywhere on the planet in any environment. They're tasked with destroying, rendering inert, anything that can go boom, from mines and shells to improvised explosive devices like the roadside bombs made infamous in places like Iraq. They work on land and underwater. And they can even render safe the world's deadliest weapons, those loaded with nuclear, chemical, or biological payloads. They do other things too, but just what is classified.

And Jon decided to run his command, one of the most demanding in the military, with Scrum. Given the nature of his work, interviews with someone like Jon are rare. Still, I sent him a list of twelve questions about Scrum and his work. He was cleared to answer nine of them over email. I don't want to put words into his mouth, so I'll share with you the email I received from him.

His response begins with this disclaimer:

> The views provided are those of the author and do not necessarily represent the views of Navy Expeditionary Combat Command, the Department of the Navy, the Department of Defense, or the United States Government.

Q. When did you first hear about Scrum?
I first heard about Scrum when I was preparing for my command tour. I was reaching out to mentors and assembling a reading list which covered many topics from leadership and management to communication and emotional intelligence.

It was through this process that I found Scrum. When I saw it, I committed to learning more by reading *Scrum: The Art of Doing Twice the Work in Half the Time*. This was approximately two years ago and began my journey learning about Agility and the Scrum framework.

Q. What inspired you to implement Scrum at EOD?
Instead of making decisions we try experiments whenever possible. These experiments have some necessary conditions to be implemented. The first is that the cost must be low and the risk must be very low. These experiments must also be temporary in nature and reversible if the experiment proves unsuccessful. Finally, there must be some metric that we can monitor to see if the experiment had the intended outcome.

Implementing Scrum met all of these requirements.

It took no money to start the experiment; there was low risk to implementing Scrum; it was temporary and could be easily reversed if it was unsuccessful; and it had metrics such as Velocity included to evaluate its effectiveness. By measuring productivity from week to week, weekly productivity can be tracked and is known as Team Velocity.

Q. How was it structured? How did you set it up?
We structured our Scrum implementation to be consistent with the Scrum framework roles, activities, and artifacts. The Scrum Master was the Executive Officer, the Product Owner was the Commanding Officer, and the Scrum Team was the remainder of key staff positions. The composition of the group changed over time as we refined our understanding of what products and services each member of the command supported.

Q. What was the impact immediately?

Team Velocity started at 4 points per day and steadily grew to 50 points per day. The immediate impact was to improve communications, prioritization, and task accomplishment.

Q. What were the elements that had the most impact? Why?

The elements that had the most impact were defining the objectives and agenda for all of the activities. While many of the activities mirrored actions that are customary in military life, they lacked the objectives and agenda clarity that they gained with our Scrum implementation.

Timeboxing also became an essential part of our daily life.

The reason that Timeboxing and understanding the objectives of every event became so vital to us is we could measure our effectiveness against common, understood, thoughtful objectives each time the Team met. This allowed us to be more focused and this focus allowed us to achieve more meaningful work.

Q. Can you give an example of something you were able to do with Scrum that you weren't before?

As a leader, I am much more attuned to the effects my actions have on the Team. By conducting rigorous Retrospectives, I know how my actions impact Team Happiness.

As an example, I pushed the Team during one Sprint to accomplish a specific objective that was out of line with some of our priorities heading into that Sprint. At the Retrospective, I asked the Team for their input and got honest feedback on how my actions had caused a steep drop in

Team Happiness. Without Scrum, the Team never would've had a mechanism to deliver that feedback to me, and I would never have known the results of my actions.

Q. What was hard? Did you have to modify anything?
It was hard to convince the Team that we needed to conduct all events in the Sprint. While there was broad acceptance of the Daily Scrum, people felt that we were spending a lot of time in meetings by doing Backlog Refinement and Retrospectives, which wasn't always appreciated. Gradually, as the Team began to understand the impact of things like having a clean and ready backlog or soliciting Team Happiness and continuous improvement suggestions at Retrospectives, the Team gained more approval and acceptance of these events.

Q. Run through your Sprint. How and where did you do each event?
The Sprint starts Monday morning when we meet with all of our platoons for our weekly synchronization meeting. This allows us to solicit feedback from all of the Teams operating within the command.

From there, we go into Sprint Planning where we can take the input we just received and incorporated into our Sprint plan. When the Sprint plan is complete, we move into Daily Scrum and discuss how we will begin our work. This is all done in our conference room.

We then have Daily Scrum in that same conference room using our Team board, which is available to anyone in the command to see. On Wednesday afternoon we meet to conduct Backlog Refinement in front of our Team board.

Backlog Refinement involves discussing and prioritizing work to be done. On Friday we have an all-hands call with our sailors to present to them the work we've accomplished. This is our Sprint Review. Friday afternoon we gather the Team for our Retrospective in front of the Team board.

Q. Will it last after you move on?
The future's impossible to know, but the groundwork is in place, and infrastructure exists for Scrum to outlive my tenure.

Now, think back on what you just read. Take out the occasional mention of rank and sailors and focus on the key points. This is not a military example; it's an example of Scrum working in a complex, difficult, and unpredictable environment.

Commander Haase and his team were always highly skilled and motivated. As Special Forces, they are the best of the best almost by default. Yet after implementing Scrum, Haase and his team saw productivity improve from 4 to 50 points a day in eighteen months. That's an increase of 1,250 percent.

And though the work they do can be high-tech, this is not the story of a software start-up, or even a team that is creating a product. In a way they are a services company with a highly specialized, dangerous, and lethal delivery. Since I worked with Jon, there has been a steady stream of Navy Special Warfare folk coming through my classes. And these are people who, above all, focus on results. There is zero tolerance for anything that doesn't make them faster and more effective.

As a former journalist, I know skepticism can be healthy. But it must be balanced with acceptance of proof. If not, then skepticism can be counterproductive, even destructive. Especially when skepticism is just a disguise for simple fear of change.

On the Edge of Chaos

In Ann Arbor, home of the University of Michigan, there was a graduate student in the early 1980s who was fascinated by the idea of modeling life inside a computer. That student, Christopher Langton, started to play about with what he called cellular automata.

Cellular automata are cells on a grid whose state evolves through time based on a set of rules. Each cell is in a neighborhood of other cells whose state influences them. The simplest neighborhood is just the cells touching a cell. And the rules can be simple: for example, if the cell next to me is on, I too turn on. To take a more complex scenario, if two of my neighbors are on and one of my neighbors is off, I turn off.

This can get pretty complicated pretty quickly. I'll spare you the math, but what Langton did was to categorize the rule sets by whether they caused a lot of change or a little change. He called that metric "lambda." The higher the lambda, the more change that the set of rules caused. A lower lambda drove less change. That's when the really interesting thing happened. If lambda is too low, the whole thing quickly becomes frozen and static. If lambda is too high, the system becomes chaotic. But right between those two states there is a phase transition. The rules can't be too strict, because that paralyzes the system, and they can't be too loose, because that drives the system into chaos. There has to be just enough structure, just barely enough, right there at the edge of chaos.

And that edge of chaos, it turns out, describes a lot of different things. It's not just mathematically and computationally interesting. It describes what has come to be called a complex adaptive system. It's where you can see the results of a system *only as it is working*. Even if you understand each part of a system completely, it is only when those parts begin to interact that you see properties emerge from the interactions. And you cannot predict what those will be.

My father says this is the epiphany that drove the creation of Scrum. He was running a large waterfall project at a bank when he read Langton's paper. It showed him, he says, why his project was years late and tens of millions of dollars over budget. Riding the edge of chaos where Langton saw the highest speed of evolution in digital life—that is what Scrum is *designed to do*.

Let me give you an example. Traffic. Every morning across the planet people, without discussing it that much with each other, leap into their cars in the hundreds of millions and race down the street on their way to work. You are one of them. Coffee in hand, you become a piece of the system known as traffic. Maybe there's an accident and someone slows down to take a look. Then the person behind them slows down a little bit more, then the next person, and soon enough you have a ripple effect that brings the whole highway to a halt. And then you decide to bail, get off the highway onto the local streets. But you're not the only one with that idea, and soon people are racing through residential streets and jamming them up. So you try a different route and discover that if you drive down that alley and slip through the grocery store parking lot, you can bypass the whole thing. This is the system, through individual action, seeking a solution.

And here's the problem about problems. It's not only cellular automata that act in complex adaptive ways; it's economics, ecology, neurology, teams, even society itself. If the rules are too strict, nothing changes. A culture fossilizes. Nothing can get done. The structure ultimately collapses. The way the Soviet Union did in the late 1980s. Stable for a long time, but a sudden collapse. But if the rules are too loose, you have chaos. Rioting in the streets. Everyone for themselves. No societal cohesion at all.

If you have just enough structure to ride that edge of chaos, that's where interesting things happen. Creativity blossoms and can be channeled. Ideas are generated and applied. There is freedom of expression but also some controls in place to focus it.

The other strange thing about this kind of system is that very small changes can be amplified in a nonlinear, dynamic way. In other words, if you change one thing, the whole system can change. This is what allows the individual elements to self-organize to solve problems dynamically. It's also what makes it impossible to determine at the beginning of a process what will happen next, although at the end it may look obvious that things should have turned out that way. Take the American Revolution as an example. Today it seems inevitable that the colonies would revolt, toss out the English, and found the United States of America. But if you read contemporary sources, no one had any *idea* that would happen. That wasn't really the plan until events overtook the colonists. And their success was a close call.

I'm reminded of how Arthur Wellesley spoke about the Battle of Waterloo, which ended the Napoleonic Era for good. He called it "the nearest run thing you ever saw in your life." In a letter he described it this way:

> The history of a battle, is not unlike the history of a ball. Some individuals may recollect all the little events of which the great result is the battle won or lost, but no individual can recollect the order in which, or the exact moment at which, they occurred, which makes all the difference as to their value or importance.

It seems obvious afterward, but no one can really recall all the individual forces that were acting. It may have been the act of one person, at one moment, who did exactly the right thing and it all turned. In an age where it can sometimes seem that individual action has no impact, I find it heartening to learn that if we touch the system just right, one person can make all the difference.

The common reaction by traditional management to complex spaces is to set up more controls—to put more rules in place in an effort to control the chaos. More stoplights. More cameras. And the whole thing grinds to a halt. Decisions simply can't be made.

Scrum is an attempt to give people a tool to manage these types of systems. Instead of trying to restrict the system, Scrum builds just enough structure, just enough rules. It can look chaotic, but it isn't. Scrum is not settled. It's subtle control. One person, or maybe every person, can contribute value.

A global oil company asked us to work with some of their teams who decided where they should drill new wells. They had an elaborate system of phase gates that the engineers had to go through. It required huge amounts of oversight, documentation, and lots and lots of meetings. When Scrum Inc.'s coaches got there and turned the teams into Scrum Teams, we told management: *Stop telling them what to do. Instead, become their mentors. Each Team Member is an individual actor, and they work together to meet their goal, which is to deliver new wells. Allow them the freedom to do it.* Sure, the Teams did need to produce some documents and conduct the right studies. But they figured out what was needed to make the decision to drill. What we had them do is talk about what they actually produced in each phase gate and put it on a wall so everyone could see it. Then, by ignoring the traditional steps and focusing instead on deliverables, they could prioritize: they could see how to work together to deliver incrementally. They took a glacial phase gate system that limited them and turned it into an actionable Agile backlog.

In Scrum, each individual on the Team contributes their thoughts, ideas, and insights. They can shape the whole thing. In a traditional structure those ideas are squashed by the system: its controls, its limits, more and more structure. The whole thing grinds to a halt.

Instead, Scrum focuses on and exploits the non-deterministic and complex system dynamics. It delivers not by centralizing the decision-making in one place but by driving it out to the nodes, where the knowledge is—to the Teams and the Product Owner—so things can actually get done without waiting. It's a complex system with a purpose. Or as Langton put it, deterministic chaos.[1]

The Perfect Is the Enemy of the Good

The real answer to whatever decision you make will only emerge from the interactions of the individual elements of the system. To quote Eisenhower again:[2]

> Plans are worthless, but planning is everything. There is a very great distinction because when you are planning for an emergency you must start with this one thing: the very definition of "emergency" is that it is unexpected, therefore it is not going to happen the way you are planning.

But people love plans (especially their own plans), so they make a lot of them. And they want the perfect plan, so they demand more reports and more data in order to make the right decision. Inevitably, though, this takes longer and longer, and instead of the goal being to reach a decision, the process of making the decision becomes the goal. There are studies and hearings and debates, but nothing actually gets done. This can go on for a long time, depending on the nature of the decision, because everyone wants the perfect plan, and they think that if they just had enough information, they could make it perfect.

Again, though, there is no perfect plan, because it is impossible to know the results of a dynamic system in advance. The only thing you can do is try *something* and get feedback. Any action is better than no action. Don't dither, do. At one level, it doesn't matter what you do; it just matters that you do, in order to learn and move forward.

What Scrum does is give you quick feedback on whether that decision was a good one or not. It allows you to pivot, to change your mind, to seek a different path, to tack toward the goal. Each quick decision informs the next. The path emerges from the doing.

In 1999, while at IBM, a guy named Dave Snowden came up with a way of looking at problems to help leaders know what kind of problem they are facing, and what kind of solution they should be looking for. He calls it the Cynefin framework—*cynefin* is a Welsh word that means "habitat"—because you need to know where you stand.

The first type of problem in Snowden's framework is *simple* or *obvious*. This is the kind of problem that has already been solved. There actually is a best practice that works all the time. Once you can determine that a problem is simple, you can apply a known recipe from your bag of tricks. If you're playing poker, never draw to an inside straight. A bank shouldn't make loans to people with x level of debt load. With simple problems, the relationship between cause and effect is not only clear but obvious.

The second type of problem is *complicated*. This is the kind of problem where you have a known unknown. Take the oil company example: when geologists run a seismic survey to learn where they could drill for oil, they know they don't know the answer, but they know how to find it. This is the domain of the expert. Once you have ascertained that the problem is solvable, you can work out a solution, even if it turns out to be tricky. If you're knowledgeable enough, you can figure out cause and effect. I always think of this when I bring my car into the shop. It's making a weird noise and

I'm worried. I know I don't know how to address this problem, but I know that my mechanic knows, or can figure it out.

The third type of problem is *complex*. This is the kind of problem we've been talking about. The ones where you can only figure out afterward why what happened happened. Here you have to take some sort of action. Here is where you need to do something to see what happens before you act again.

Complex problems are the kind of problems most of us wrestle with. All the time. The answers are not known, and all the forces aren't known. But we have to do something. And what happens will surprise you.

Let me tell you the story of Twitch. If you don't know what it is, it's a web service that allows people to stream themselves playing a videogame so that other people can watch them do it. This is not an obvious product except in retrospect. But Twitch is an incredible success story. Amazon acquired it for $970 million in 2014.

This company's first product idea? A calendar that would integrate with Gmail. Of course, then Google came out with Google Calendar. So the company decided to go into livestreaming. One of the founders would stream his entire life, 24/7. Camera on head, big backpack with a computer. Constantly live. They built an incredibly fast livestreaming service that a lot of people could use at the same time. But as it turns out, no one really wanted to watch that livestream. So they opened the idea up—maybe people wanted to livestream themselves? It really wasn't working in the marketplace, and they were running out of cash. Then they noticed that a lot of people were watching livestreams of people playing videogames. Weird. But they went with that, and it turns out there is an avid audience of fans and recreational videogamers who want to watch the top players play. People can make a small fortune just playing videogames and streaming it for others to watch.

That's an extreme example of a solution to a need no one knew existed. But the problems we are facing today in business, in politics, and in society are tough ones. Often we simply do not know the solution. And sometimes we don't know how to even approach the solution.

So what you need to do is try *something* and then see what happens. Take the results of that and tweak what you are doing. Then try again. Tweak again. And let the solution emerge. That's what Scrum is: a series of small experiments in short periods of time to find a solution to a complex problem.

The final type of problem in the Cynefin framework is *chaotic*. This is a crisis. As Eisenhower said, you can't plan for emergencies. What is needed to address an emergency is quick and sure action from leadership. Let's say there is a tsunami, or an oil rig blows up, or an uprising turns into a revolution, or there's a stock market crash. The first thing to do is to take action quickly, and begin to take steps to encapsulate the problem, to define its limits, to bring it out of the chaotic and into the realm of the merely complex. One example I use to describe this kind of problem is a riot. One night during the Arab Spring I was in the middle of a crowd that decided to storm the parliament building, or something like that. Anyway, this crowd of tens of thousands lurched as one toward the parliament gates. Then screams broke out from one side. This is when the crowd got chaotic, everyone running around unsure of what to do, and they turned from individuals into a mob. I was standing in the middle of this with a young American student I'd hired because she spoke Arabic. I told her, and I'll tell you, what to do in a riot. First, don't panic. I cannot emphasize how important that is. Blind fear is what gets people trampled and killed. Second, find something hard that can't easily be knocked over. Like a lamppost or something. It's bizarre—the crowd will part around you like a river around a stone. What you've done is pulled the chaotic into the complex. Take a minute. Breathe. Figure out what the escape routes are. You have that freedom now. You can't do anything when you're just another body being flung about, but if you can get out of the noise and fear, you can start to come up with a plan.

Here speed matters. Delaying the decision will only worsen the problem. By rapidly iterating—trying something, seeing the response, trying again—you can ultimately succeed in bringing the crisis under control. This trial-and-error approach can feel terrifying in the moment. But it is also an opportunity. New ways of doing things will emerge as people try to figure out how to work in an environment that didn't exist the day before.

Chaos. Uncertainty. Action.

On the morning of September 11, 2001, Kenneth Holden and his deputy Michael Burton were the leaders of an obscure bureaucracy deep within city government, the Department of Design and Construction (DDC). They oversaw the construction contracts for street repairs, libraries, courthouses—the physical nuts and bolts of a city as mammoth as New York. On that fateful Tuesday morning no one knew what to do after the planes hit the World Trade Center. The city's much-ballyhooed Office of Emergency Management didn't act. All Holden and Burton knew was that they had to get huge amounts of equipment and expertise to the World Trade Center site to start digging through the wreckage—to search for survivors and to clean up the gargantuan pile of debris that remained.

They had no grand strategy. They were only thinking a few hours in advance. They really shouldn't have been involved at all, but they started making calls to construction companies they knew from previous contracts. They had lights brought in that very night so the rescue efforts could continue in the darkness. They bypassed all the normal rules and procedures and chose four construction companies they knew to start the work.

At first the Police and Fire Departments resisted them. But the two just kept making decisions: *Is this building safe to search? Probably.* Normally this kind of disaster is federalized by the Federal Emergency Management Agency and the Army Corps of Engineers. But this time, when the federal agencies asked what was happening, they were told what was being done—and were told to keep out of it. Burton wasn't asking anyone for permission.

And they were so effective, they got so much done, they coordinated the massive project so well that Mayor Rudolph Giuliani told the other city agencies, the ones that were supposed to be in charge, to back off and let the DDC run the show. They set up a command center in a kindergarten classroom, as William Langiewiesche recounted in his excellent book *American Ground: Rebuilding the World Trade Center*:

> No one had time to ponder options and write plans. It was action, pure action, that was called for. Because of the need for clear communication, Burton instituted large twice-daily meetings in one of the kindergarten rooms—a simple, low-tech management system that proved to be particularly well suited to the apocalypse outside. Burton's reasoning was lucid as usual. To me, he said, "The only way we can get control of the situation is by having everyone here. There's no time for distributing memos or waiting for the chain of command. Everybody has to hear what the problems are. The decisions have to be made, and everybody has to hear about those decisions. We have to keep everyone moving in the same direction.

Michael Burton went on to be known as the "Trade Center czar." He defined, shaped, and coordinated how three thousand people removed 1.5 million tons of rubble, ash, and steel in less than a year. Action, pure action, is what is required to pull a chaotic situation into a complex one.

The key lesson here is in almost every circumstance, the first thing to figure out is where you are, and then start running experiments to see if you are, actually, where you think you are. Make a decision; don't wait. Those who dawdle are overtaken by events. Those who act seize the opportunities created by them.

Don't Let the Shadows Fool You

Most people don't even think about the time factor. They don't understand that every moment is precious. Once it's gone, you can't get it back. They aren't aware that every time they wait, they are making failure or delay ever more likely. If you can do one thing, just one, make sure you have a Daily Scrum with everyone who is needed to make decisions on what you're doing. Something as simple as getting together will drive decision latency down dramatically. And the more decisions you don't have to make, by empowering your Teams and Product Owners to make them instead, the faster the decision-making process will be. It's a simple thing, but you will start to become an organization that lets those who know the most about a problem decide how to fix it.

Let's use another Napoleonic example: Napoleon Bonaparte's Grande Armée, which rolled across Europe like a wave, victory after victory, conquering the continent in just a few years. Back then, when some unit of soldiers saw the enemy, the general rule was not to engage but to send word back to headquarters to ask what to do. Napoleon changed all that with two simple rules. One: *If you see the enemy, start shooting.* Two: *Ride toward the sound of the guns!* Those two rules allowed tens of thousands of French troops to self-organize and bring the whole weight of their forces to where the action was without asking anyone for permission or direction.

One unit would start firing, the units nearby would ride toward them and start shooting as well, and it would spread like wildfire, more and more French forces putting pressure on exactly the place where it was needed. Those two rules changed warfare forever.

Don't wait. Act.

> ## THE TAKEAWAY
>
> ***Don't wait to make a decision***. One hour. That's the goal. That's how fast decisions need to be made. Waiting for the committee to decide is entering into a suicide pact with destiny. If it is taking more than five hours to make a decision, that's almost surely a sign that you had to send it up a chain for approval.
>
> ***Empower the right decision-makers***. That's the key. Only the people who actually have the most knowledge and understand the most about a situation should make the decision. That's how you do it fast. The solutions to problems lie not in the heads of management but with those who have direct contact with customers, out in the nodes.
>
> ***Keep rules to a minimum***. If the rules are too unbending, nothing changes. A culture fossilizes. Nothing can get done. But if you have just enough structure to ride that edge of chaos, that's where interesting things happen.
>
> ***Manage complexity with simplicity***. Simple rules generate complex adaptive behavior. Complex rules leave only space for simple, stupid behavior. Scrum has just enough structure, just enough rules. It can look chaotic, but it isn't. Scrum is not settled. It's subtle control.

BACKLOG

- Next time you have a meeting to make decisions, run a clock and add up the cost of that meeting. Include salaries of those in attendance. How much time is wasted waiting for a decision to be made?

- Think about the last time you or your organization faced a crisis. Could you have acted more quickly? Or were you surprised at how quickly the organization moved and responded? How could you change your decision-making process next time?

- What is the absolute minimum you can do to get the results you want? What can you stop doing?

- Think about a complicated gatekeeping system you have to deal with every day. If you focused on value instead of process, what would it look like?

CHAPTER 4

Busy vs. Done

Confirmation.com is a company created to solve a problem that wasted thousands of hours and millions of trees each year. They took a manual process that was slow and painful and hard and made it electronic, fast, and easy.

What they do is confirm financial data through a huge global network of accounting firms, financial institutions, law firms, and corporations. They think it should be easy to find the truth. And they realize that financial fraud isn't going away, which is why the motto of their founder, Brian Fox, is that they help the good guys catch the bad guys.

Let me give you just one illustrative example. The founder and chairman of Peregrine Financial Group, Russell Wassendorf Sr., defrauded investors out of more than $200 million over a period of years. How did he do it? A little Photoshop and he was able to create real-looking bank statements. The whole thing came tumbling down when Peregrine was forced to begin using Confirmation

.com. Within days the fraud became clear. And Wassendorf still has decades left in jail for his crimes.

For more than a hundred years, the confirmation process was done on paper. An auditor would send confirmation requests by mail to a bank: *Does the institution being audited actually have this much money?* The bank would receive not only this request but thousands of others—even hundreds of thousands—each year. Banks had to have whole groups of people deal with it. Each confirmation request needed to be responded to by manually checking the bank records, writing a letter that confirmed the institution had that much money, and sending it back by mail. Paper. Lots and lots of paper. It took *weeks* for each and every one of the many, many tens of thousands of these requests made each year.

Confirmation.com made all this happen in a matter of moments. When someone makes a request, Confirmation.com directs that request to one of the thousands of connected banks in its network, gets the response, and passes it back to the auditor. The amount of security needed to move all that sensitive financial data around is critical. And that was the hard part in the beginning: getting financial institutions, accounting firms, law firms, and their mutual clients to trust the Confirmation.com system.

Confirmation.com pioneered the idea of electronic confirmations almost twenty years ago—receiving seven patents along the way—and is still dominant in the space by a large margin. It started with one bank and one accounting firm in Nashville, Tennessee, and now sixteen thousand accounting firms, four thousand banks, and five thousand law firms in 160 countries use their platform. They confirm more than a trillion dollars of assets each year.

When the company started back in 2000, at first it was just four people, literally in a garage, cranking out their product, this new thing that had never been done before, which Brian envisioned and wrote up as his entrepreneurship paper in business school. Eventually big banks started to realize the amount of work they would save and the speed they would gain, and ultimately said they would only accept requests through Confirmation.com's platform—no more paper. Confirmation.com grew rapidly, and they started to add new features and new confirmation types—like legal confirmations—to their platform.

But then something happened. They weren't getting things done quickly enough. They were missing deadlines. The code quality a platform like theirs requires wasn't there. They certainly weren't going to risk that, so they took more time to try to get it right. Oh, they had people working hard. They were busy. One executive there told us he had to keep everyone busy. Hopefully they'd get something done, but if they didn't, he could at least say he tried. But they were simply unable to get stuff out the door. Everyone was busy, but not much was getting done. So they called us.

This is a fairly typical issue in corporations. Some project—it doesn't matter what it is—must get done. Management or sales or somebody has said it's a top priority. Then someone else says something else is also a top priority. And someone else brings in yet another. And, of course, none of these people insisting that their priority is what everyone should focus on talk to one another. They just keep shoving them down on the teams. This is horrifyingly commonplace. Then, with the predictability of gravity, things stop getting done. So management starts putting pressure on the team. They want them to be busy all the time working on the many, many things that are all top priority. They make them work nights and weekends to meet an arbitrary deadline that they promised to someone. And they are mystified when it doesn't happen.

Facts Can Be Stubborn Things

Priority is an old word. It began its life in the late fourteenth century when the French borrowed a Latin word to indicate the state of being earlier—this event happened before that event. It entered English in the early fifteenth century, referring to precedence in right or rank. (Incidentally, it's a singular word. Saying something is a "top priority" is redundant. It's using two words to say one thing. Another linguistic tidbit: Latin words aren't pluralized by putting an *s* on the end, so the word *priorities* is actually nonsensical. It quite literally does not make any sense. It's like saying there were five first-place finishers in a race.)

If you run a Google Ngram search (that's where Google looks at however many thousands of books over the past few hundred years and counts how often words are used) on *priorities*, you get the following result:

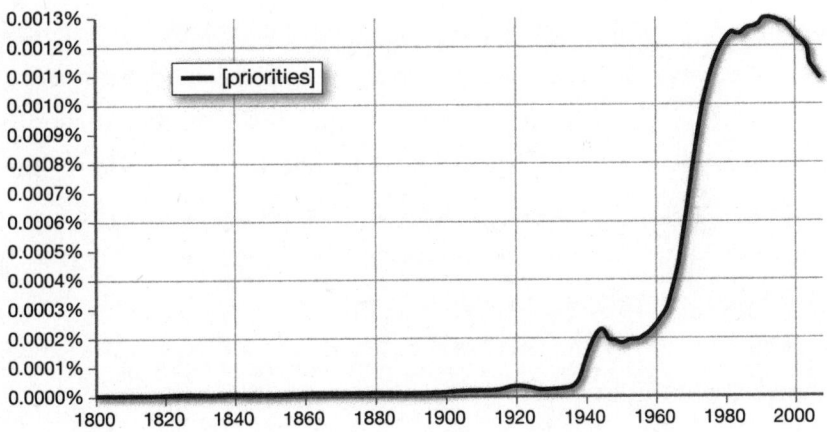

Priorities wasn't even a word until about 1940. I'm not dead certain about causation, but there is a certain correlation between the rise of the modern management movement of postwar industry and the birth of a new word that sounds seemingly logical and rigorous while actually being meaningless. That seems telling to me.

Stop Starting, Start Finishing

When Scrum Inc. goes into a company to assess how Agile they are, we usually find that about 30 percent of the work being done should not be done at all. That work is actually in *opposition* to goals of the business. Stop that. The Standish Group data says, and this is what we find, that 64 percent of the remaining 70 percent are working on features that the customer rarely or never uses. That means 75 percent of people in a company are either actively working against the business interests or are working on things that no one wants. Let that sink in for a second. Three-quarters of your company shouldn't be doing what they are doing.

The reason for this is that people refuse, or don't know how, to prioritize. (Another quick linguistic factoid: Apparently *prioritize* wasn't a word until it was first made up by government bureaucrats in the 1950s and popularized in the presidential campaign of 1972 when political operatives had to choose which voting districts to target. As the *Oxford English Dictionary* put it in 1982, it is "a word that at present sits uneasily in the language." It apparently sits uneasily in people's practices as well.)

Here are the symptoms we see. If you hear or utter any of these phrases, you might want to rethink your approach:

"We have multiple conflicting priorities."

"Our teams are constantly disrupted by new priorities."

"Everything is the number one priority."

The thing that kills me is that everyone knows these are bad things. Not a single person I have ever spoken to thinks that working on five things at once and disrupting even that work for new urgent things is a good idea. No one. We all know it's stupid. But we all do it anyway.

At Confirmation.com, everyone had different priorities. Sales wanted a better Japanese translation so they could sell there, marketing wanted to rebrand the website, and the leadership was concerned with an upstart competitor. So what should the product teams focus on? "I'm always waiting to hear what the new rules are today," one executive told Avi Schneier, Scrum Inc.'s principal on the case. When Avi asked what the company's number one priority was, he was told, "Meeting deadlines." Not what needed to be done, notice, just the deadline itself.

So Avi had them work through the company's real priorities. What are they? What is the most important thing? He helped them see that without choosing those priorities, they ended up with a company adrift, going in a different direction each day. So they made those choices. It can be done, but it requires honest reflection and some tough decisions.

Output vs. Outcome

Let's tease these two ideas apart. Output is how much stuff the Team produces each Sprint, their Velocity. When you start out with Scrum you want that Velocity to double or triple within a few months. If you can't get things out the door, even if they are the wrong things, nothing else matters. Focus on getting the Team's work to *done* and out the door. If it turns out to be the wrong thing, and it probably will be, you will find out quickly rather than wasting millions of dollars and years of your life before finding out no one wants what you are making.

But the good news is, once you know that, you can focus on outcomes. *How do we make happy customers? Save more lives? Bring value to the world?* You need to answer those questions, otherwise your work is in vain. What you want to do is get stuff in front of people so they can tell you what they love, want, and need.

The trick to doing that is getting quick feedback from whoever is getting value from what you are creating. Find out just how valuable it is to them. At the beginning of a project or product, you pretty much guess what things will be most valuable. It's an educated guess, backed up with research and the like, but still just a guess. If you have to wait six months to find out if your guess was right, well, you are planning with hope instead of data.

At Confirmation.com, their biggest problem was their legacy system. It worked, and it worked well. But as it grew over the years, it slowly accreted new features every time a customer asked for one, fixing this system or enhancing that piece. Each bit was tacked on without much thought about architecture and structure. It eventually grew into a mess so big they spent more time fixing old mistakes than building a new system to replace it. What they eventually realized is that while everyone was really busy, they weren't actually making significant forward progress. They couldn't get anything out the door efficiently. By being focused on making sure people were busy, the output, they didn't look at the outcome. They really needed a new, more modern system that would allow them to provide their customers a service that was even better than what they thought they wanted. But everyone was working on keeping the old system together—output, not outcome.

Definition of *Done* and the Nature of Architecture

The key to getting to done is defining up front what *done* actually means. When a Team picks up an item from their Product Backlog, they should know the nature of done for that piece, they need to define *done*. Part of that definition has to be how that piece builds on other pieces. Why? Because—and this is critical—the architecture of your product determines what your Definition of Done can be.

Let me give you a couple of examples. One is from the world of hardware, the other from software, but the thinking is exactly the same.

There is a private space company that will only let me call them the Stealth Space Company. That's what they called themselves on their LinkedIn page, in any of the very unwanted press coverage, and have repeatedly driven into everyone's mind. *We don't brag, we don't talk, we just do.* They're based in an abandoned naval air station sitting on the edge of San Francisco Bay. Military bases like this one do vary somewhat from location to location and service to service, but they all share one thing in common: a brutal, uncompromising architecture of function over form.

Chris Kemp is the CEO. He has blond hair, wears mainly black T-shirts, black jackets, and black pants. His mantra is speed. From his email announcing their first launch attempt:

> On Sunday, we will attempt to launch a rocket that was designed from scratch by a team that did not exist 18 months ago. We have done this five times faster, and with five times less capital, than ever before. This is the first in a series of test launches that will allow us to iterate towards orbit as we build our team and incorporate what we learn from each attempt.

He looks at Elon Musk's SpaceX and sees a target that not only can be beaten but can be beaten soundly—five times as fast at a fifth of the cost. And he is using Scrum to do it. His goal is to be the FedEx to space, launching small payloads daily into low orbit. The military needs a constellation of spy satellites over a new trouble zone? No problem; it'll be there in thirty minutes instead of three years.

Speaking with his people, you can feel their drive to succeed. One of his leaders spent his career in the space business: SpaceX, Virgin Galactic, Boeing. He said some of his team felt the whole Scrum framework is only for software.

"This is all new to me, J.J.," he told me. "But I've seen just how bad the old way of doing things is. I tell these new engineers that they don't know how good they have it, and I'm all in. I have made it very clear they're all in too, or they need to find another job."

A rocket, I learned there, is really three systems: an engine, which turns fuel into force; avionics, which directs where the rocket goes; and structures, the wrapper that holds everything together. In the first iteration of the rocket, those pieces were tightly coupled, both within each system and between systems. The reason for this is that they are trying to get rid of any excess weight, so each interface is custom-designed with custom pieces and custom connectors. Which makes sense when you are thinking only about weight. But the tricky part is when you want to fix something.

Let me give you a simple example. In their first rocket the avionics system was controlled by a series of specialized circuit boards individually connected to each other and to the rocket as a whole with switches made from some ultra-rare unobtanium material. If one board failed, you had to pull out all the boards and then redo hundreds of connections by hand with these incredibly expensive materials. At one point, the rare-earth elements used in those connections simply went off the market: Apple and Samsung had gobbled up the world stockpile for use in their next generation of phones. It took twelve weeks to get more. Kemp's reaction to this news was both profane and exasperated: "Three months for an Ethernet switch? This is the kind of [stuff] that will kill us!"

My colleague Joe Justice sat down with Ethan, the head of avionics, and talked through the problem. *First,* said Joe, *you have all of these boards with all these special connectors, each one different from the last, each carrying different information. And you need to unravel the complexity, replace them with better designs. But if you pull one, you break all the others. So let's put a stable interface between the avionics and the rest of the rocket. Let's overengineer it so that it can carry all sorts of data, more than you need, but it will use common connectors you can buy off the shelf for pennies. Let's encapsulate the problem, making a firewall of sorts that we know won't change, and let's make sure the rest of the rocket engineers know their systems only have to connect to this interface with one side of this connector and the avionics engineers know they just have to connect to the other. That way you can change anything you want on either side; as long as that interface remains the same, it doesn't matter. What you are trying to do is modularize the problems. You want it to be like Lego. You can snap the pieces together and snap them apart easily.*

This approach makes the Definition of Done easy: it has to work, and it has to fit into this known stable interface. Then you can start knocking out your problems one by one. The extra weight from the interface itself? You can iterate on that later, once you've fixed your other problems.

Now let's take an example of Agile Architecture from software. It's exactly the same pattern. Spotify is a music streaming service. Their goal, like the goal of the rocket company, is speed. When they were a start-up, the CEO of Spotify, Daniel Ek, once told Scrum Inc., "Listen, Apple, Google, and Amazon want to kill us. And they are smart, large companies with lots of skill. The only way we can survive is speed. We have to be faster than them."

So Spotify is split up into different modules, just like a rocket ship. There's the player, there's the recommendation engine, there's the playlist functionality, there's the mobile app, and so on. And just like at the Stealth Space Company, they've developed stable interfaces between each of those pieces. The teams working on the playlists can innovate as much as they want, change as much as they want, as long as it still fits within the right size box, has the same data going back and forth, and doesn't break anything else. That way they can go fast without worrying about breaking other parts of the system.

They don't have to change the whole system to change their piece of the system. That interface spares them a huge amount of pain. In many systems, the dependencies between the various pieces are so great that making any changes becomes nearly impossible, and the speed of development slows to a crawl as engineers have to use ever more duct tape and baling wire to hold an increasingly rickety and rigid system together.

Most defects, no matter what kind of product or service or process you are creating or doing, come when two perfectly good parts of the system are integrated, and to fix either one you have to break them both. It becomes exhausting.

The Fix

So what do you do? You have dozens of projects, hundreds of priorities, and they all have to get done, or so you've told yourself.

The first step, as always, is to admit you have a problem. If your strategy is to say nonsensically that everything is a priority, then what you are really saying is your strategy will be decided by the most junior person in the organization when that person, given zero guidance on what is actually most important, decides what to do next.

In using Scrum, the first thing is to make sure that every Team has a clear and ordered backlog for every single Sprint and that they understand the relative business value of everything they are being asked to do. This requires a mechanism, which I'll get into in later chapters, that takes the big goals of your organization and breaks them down into actionable items for the Team.

At Confirmation.com, Avi and another colleague, Alex Sheive, sat everyone down in a room and got all the things they wanted to do up on a wall. They worked with management to create a clear, ordered backlog for the Teams. They convinced them to keep the Teams stable, not to move people around, and they sent that message throughout the organization. Management was behind Scrum and was willing to do the hard work. They were taking a hard look at the list of things they wanted to accomplish and deciding what they were *not* going to do in order to get done what actually needed to get done.

That's the first step, admitting that you aren't going to get everything done right away. You have to make a choice. It can be hard at times. There are often a lot of competing interests. But if leadership isn't aligned with what must be done and in what order, the Teams will have no idea what to do. The leadership at Confirmation.com was able to pull it off. They restructured, they streamlined, and they made sure each Team had a clean, prioritized backlog for each and every Sprint. And it dramatically changed what they were capable of doing.

The Importance of No

The root cause of this lack of willingness to prioritize comes down to this, the unwillingness to say no. Just as every Team has a Velocity, every organization does as well: how much can we create in how much time? It is very easy to say yes to customers, to leadership, to bosses. *You want that done? No problem—we'll put it on our ever-growing backlog of things to do. Oh, and it's really important? Well, I'll just cram it in here at the top.* Then someone else asks about a project of theirs. And the answer is yes—again, always yes, until the team or the organization implodes.

Corporate strategy almost always focuses far too much on what a company will do rather than what a company won't do. Let me illustrate this. There is a global materials company that does huge amounts of research and then turns that research into everyday products manufactured at scale, with millions and millions of units going out the door. But they have a problem. This company spends years doing R&D, coming up with a new product with novel materials, and once they introduce the product, a group of what are known as "fast followers" replicate it quickly, sometimes in a matter of months. So they have to keep coming up with new products.

One particular division simply couldn't get new products into the market quickly enough. They had grand ideas but it just wasn't happening. So they called up Scrum Inc., and in early 2016 a mild-mannered guy by the name of Steve Daukas walked into that building to see what he could do.

He got the lab leadership into a room and said, "To start with, let's just talk about what you are doing. Let's get every single project on Post-it notes and on a wall so we can take a look."

A quarter hour of furious scribbling later, they had the projects on a wall. There were over a hundred of them.

"Okay," said Steve, "just for fun, let's put names on all those projects. Who is actually working on them?"

Even at only a few people a project, they ran out of names somewhere around number seventy.

"Why are you working on so many things?" asked Steve.

The answer he got was that corporate was telling them to get more products into market, so they had to do a bunch of products at once to start monetizing them quickly.

"And are any of those actually getting done?"

There was complete silence.

I have heard variants of that conversation with everyone from parents of small children to start-ups to Fortune 500 companies. They have to get so much stuff done, so they start a whole myriad of projects. In their minds, they have to; there is just so much to do. And then they can report, "Look at all of the things we are doing! We are so busy, it's crazy! We're working on all of these top priorities."

What they are actually doing is *starting* a whole bunch of things. What they aren't doing is *finishing* them. It is amazing to me to ask a company how much stuff they have in flight and they brag about it. They seem to think I will be impressed by all they are doing.

And when we ask them what impact they are having, their faces fall.

In that boardroom Steve forced the group to acknowledge that not everything was going to get done. And not only was not everything going to get done, if they continued down the path they were on, *nothing* would get done.

So they took those hundred-plus projects and started making the hard choices of what they were not going to do. What did they want their lab Teams to focus on? What would actually make a difference in the market? They argued. They lobbied. They killed people's pet projects. And they worked hard doing what leadership really has to do, which is to make choices. It is so easy to say yes to another project, so easy to agree with someone else that their idea should be pursued, so easy not to have the hard conversation. So easy not to say no.

Eventually they got down to twelve. Then Steve had the leadership of the group make clear backlogs for all of those projects. Not extremely detailed, but at a high level that communicated the "commander's intent": not how the Teams would accomplish those projects, but what and why. Next the twelve people who would be Product Owners got up in front of the whole group of scientists, a couple hundred people, and presented their backlogs—what they were trying to accomplish, why it was important, and what skills they needed to deliver it. And then the Product Owners and management left the room, telling everyone, *You're smart—you figure out who should be on which Team to accomplish those twelve goals.*

Thirty minutes later, they went back in. All of the backlogs had a Team or Teams, except for one. That one involved some tedious government compliance documentation updates they had to do but no one wanted to do it. Eventually one brave soul raised his hand and said, Fine, I'll do it. It has to be done—let's see how fast we can get this done.

In ten weeks they doubled their productivity, discovered revenue opportunities they never would have before, and crushed some fifty-three impediments raised by the Teams getting in their way. A structural reorganization emerged as the goal shifted from output (making sure everyone was busy) to outcome (getting to done). And the results were remarkable. Their typical development life cycle was two and a half years; with Scrum they had two new products in six weeks. And they had customers, big ones, who wanted to buy their product right away. That's what focus can do. They went from a hundred projects not getting done to twelve that did—twelve projects that changed the fate of the division and impacted the stock price of their multibillion-dollar corporate parent.

Focusing on getting things *done* has impact. Just say no.

Don't Be Busy, Be Done

The human brain quite literally cannot multitask. An especially apt example is that daily practice of multitasking: driving and talking on a cellphone. The research is very clear on this. People who drive while talking on cellphones—even those of the hands-free variety—get into more accidents than people who don't. The problem is especially alarming when you consider that, according to the National Highway Transportation Safety Administration, at any given moment 8 percent of people on the road are talking on their cellphone.

That is what multitasking has bequeathed us. Here's a quote from my favorite paper on the subject:

> Even when participants direct their gaze at objects in the driving environment, they often fail to "see" them when they are talking on a cell phone because attention has been directed away from the external environment and toward an internal, cognitive context associated with the phone conversation.[1]

People will actually look at an object—the car they're about to rear-end or the tree they're about to wrap their car around—and not see it. Yet we persist in driving and talking on the phone.

Whenever you attempt to do more than one thing at a time, you lose a huge amount of your productive capability to what's called context switching loss. There are studies that show that just answering an email can derail your brain for half an hour before you can get back in the right headspace for the work you are doing.

Consider this: How many times have you been interrupted while reading this book? How about while reading this chapter? Heck, did someone text you while you were reading this page? Did you just look for your phone after reading that? Did you read the messages you've missed while reading this chapter? We live in a society that expects us to respond immediately to interruptions. If you don't respond to that email or Slack message or text right away, you are insulting the person who reached out and poked you, demanding your attention. How many times yesterday did you stop what you were doing with people right in front of you to respond electronically to someone not in the room? And at the end of the day, what you began still isn't finished, you still haven't gotten back to that other really important email, and there's that thing you were going to do that was really important but now you can't remember what it was. And then you turn to the task you were supposed to be working on but now you have no idea what you were thinking or where you were headed. And don't you need to go pick up the kids now anyway?

There's actually been quite a bit of research on this—people quite literally cannot multitask. Put people in fMRI machines and ask them to do a few things at once, and you see that their brains just can't handle it. But by making choices, by saying no, by prioritizing clearly, you can change your fate. That global manufacturer did. Confirmation.com did. The Stealth Space Company launched its first rocket. There are ways of surviving and even thriving in this rapidly changing world we live in. But it does require some real insights, and some real choices. The first one, as I'll explain in Chapter 5, is asking whether you are controlled by your fear or by your hope. *You* get to decide. Even if you think things are out of control. Even if you believe the forces acting on you and on your organization are immutable. Even if you're looking at the onrushing edge of a cliff, you get to decide what you're going to do about it.

It isn't always easy. But as you'll see, fear really is the mindkiller. And the antidote is connection.

THE TAKEAWAY

Admit you have a priority problem. If your strategy is to say nonsensically that everything is a priority, then what you are really saying is your strategy will be decided by any person in the organization who, given zero guidance on what is *actually* most important, decides what to do next.

Get to done. The key to getting to done is defining up front what done actually means. When a Team picks up an item from their Product Backlog, they should know the nature of done for that piece, but also how that piece builds on other pieces. Your architecture determines what your definition of done *can* be.

Don't confuse being busy with being done. Focusing on utilization as the metric keeps people busy, but it doesn't lead to anything actually being delivered. Don't focus on outputs; focus on outcomes.

Know the power of no. Corporate strategy typically focuses far too much on what a company will do rather than what a company won't do. Choices have to be made.

BACKLOG

- Write down all your priorities and put them on a wall in a single column. Order them in terms of value, risk, and effort. But remember, it is a single list and a single column. If you have multiple priorities at any stage, reprioritize your list.

- What is your definition of done? Write it down. Put it on a wall where you can see it every day.

- Come up with three ways you could better measure outcomes versus outputs. Find at least one person to ask about the impact your work is having or the amount you are doing.

- What is the architecture of your product? Is it tightly coupled or modular? Where could you insert a known stable interface so that breaking one thing doesn't break another?

CHAPTER 5

People and Places That Seem Crazy Usually Are

Why people act in ways that seem slightly mad and repeatedly don't drive through the results they are looking for is simple: fear. And trust me on this one, because I know fear. I know its curves and special places, its harsh planes, its acrid taste, its shuddering caress, and its dark seduction.

I spent much of my adult life in war zones working as a journalist for NPR. When people find out, they inevitably ask, "What is it like?" For a few years I resented the question. But I came to realize that they quite honestly just wanted some sense of what it felt like to be in a situation they will hopefully never know. I finally came up with a stock answer: incredibly terrifying and horribly loud.

One night in Benghazi I couldn't sleep. It was 2011, and not being able to sleep wasn't terribly unusual, mainly because the good citizens of Benghazi, flush with revolutionary fervor and carrying the fruits of looting every armory they could find, thought that not shooting a gun you were carrying was downright unpatriotic. So they shot them off into the air at every opportunity, apparently unaware that high-velocity rounds don't simply vanish into the ether. My bullet-holed window bore testament to that. That night they were really digging deep.

Libya was just the latest stop on my revolutionary tour. I was on assignment as a senior producer for NPR. I'd produced our coverage of the Arab Spring since the beginning, and the powers that be on the foreign desk thought that after revolutionary Cairo, Libya was a natural follow-on for Lourdes Garcia-Navarro and me. Neither of us had been home for more than a few days in months.

I'd been through enough bang-bang in various wars, insurgencies, and insurrections over the years that I became pretty good at ID'ing weapons by their sound: the sharp stutter of an AK-47, the rolling throaty choke of a .50-caliber machine gun, the darker and more ominous thumps of mortars, all the way up to artillery, rockets, tanks, and (my personal best) twenty thousand pounds of JDAMs (joint direct attack munitions—or, more simply, really big bombs) the Israelis dropped on one building in Beirut, an explosion that quite literally blew me out of bed. But in Libya, Qaddafi had apparently had a taste for esoteric weapons, because I saw and heard guns that I couldn't recognize. That night, as the city erupted in gunfire and lit up as if there was a battle of epic proportions rolling down every street, my brain kept insisting that something was wrong—not because a bunch of idiots were blasting away with military weapons in a crowded city, but because the sounds were wrong.

The Libyans were celebrating the capture or torture or death or something of one of Qaddafi's sons—I wasn't quite sure, and knew I wouldn't be for a while. Libya just depressed me. Sure, Qaddafi was a bad guy, but you could see the signs of bloody anarchy even back then, while the civil war was still going on: militia groups suddenly realizing their weapons gave them real power, checkpoints set up as extortion, growing numbers of radicals, the settling of old scores, ethnic revenge, the whole kit and caboodle of a society tearing at its own flesh. I'd seen it before, but in Libya it seemed like it was fast-forwarding from liberation to Mogadishu in weeks, not the months or years it usually takes.

I was chatting with Arnold Strong, a Ranger buddy of mine, over Facebook. We'd met in Kandahar in 2006 when he was a major, and we'd hit it off; we remain good friends to this day. "I hate war," I wrote. "It takes the darkest places in the human heart and gives them value."

"Is it just war that does that?" he replied. Arnold knew war. We had spent a summer bouncing around southern Afghanistan together. I'll never forget the gruff, giant Ranger tenderly getting me to eat breakfast as I shook with fear one morning. NPR was sending me to another hot spot. To get there I'd have to travel down a road being hit regularly with airstrikes. He knew war, and he knew fear, and he knew me.

"That is a very good question," I typed back.

A Ramshackle Palace of Mind

To explain fear, I need to talk about memory just for a second. Whenever you experience something, it is packed up inside your brain. And however you feel about that, good or ill, is handled by a small almond-shaped group of nuclei deep in the brain called the amygdala. This happens without any sort of cognitive function. The emotional response happens first.

The weird thing about memory is that every time you recall something, you change the memory itself. You're remembering for the first time, every time. This is a great survival mechanism. By allowing newer experiences to color our past memories, we are not trapped in being the same person we were when we first experienced it. We change and grow and can move on from trauma.

On the morning of September 11, 2001, Elizabeth Phelps had just reached her office when the second plane hit the World Trade Center. She watched one of the towers go down from a window. Like most people on that day, she couldn't believe it. She left work. She watched CNN all day. She tried to give blood. Like so many people on that day, she felt paralyzed and wanted to do something.

But Dr. Phelps isn't a first responder or a soldier or a journalist. She researches memory. She is especially interested in how emotion and memory are linked. So she and colleagues across the country decided to survey people about their memories immediately after 9/11. By September 18 they had set up interview tables across Manhattan. And then they also distributed thousands of questionnaires across the country. Some sample questions:

1. Please describe how you first became aware of the terrorist attack on America.

2. What time was it on the East Coast when you first became aware of the attack?

3. How did you first learn about it (what was the source of the information)?

4. Where were you?

5. What were you doing?

6. Who else was there?

7. How did you feel when you first became aware of the attack?

The questionnaire finished up by asking how confident people were in those memories.

The researchers did the survey again a year later. Then three years later. Then ten. Fascinatingly, what happened was that while people's memories became less and less accurate over time, their confidence in those memories remained quite high. As Dr. Phelps told *Scientific American*:

> If you look at memory for 9/11, pretty much everybody would say, "I know where I was, who I was with," etc. etc. Everyone thinks, "Oh, I never would forget that." But we know from a lot of studies from the past 30 years that people aren't necessarily right. You can't even convince people that their memories are wrong. All you can say is that data would suggest your memory's wrong.
>
> With emotional events like 9/11, I think we do have a better memory for the important details [as compared with a neutral event]—we just don't have a great memory for all the details. And we think we do, and that's the real contrast. Whereas, if I told you that you don't remember the details of your 26th birthday, you wouldn't be surprised, necessarily.

So that's memory. The most powerful memories, what are called "flashbulb" memories, change—they lose their emotional impact, or at the very least the impact changes and evolves. That's a good thing. Because if they didn't, we would always carry our wounds with us. The terror we felt that day would never dim, never recede, never become part of our history rather than remaining our present.

The problem is sometimes fear rearranges a small piece of your brain and you can't forget how it feels. This little piece of neural structure, the amygdala, tells you when you are afraid. The hard part, though, is that it can control your mental state. It can tell you you are afraid. And in doing so it colors not only what you think but how you think and what you are *capable* of thinking.

What are we all afraid of in our work lives? Well, that we might not have a job or a work life anymore. That we might not have a company to work for anymore.

And that's absolutely rational. The average life span of a company has been diminishing for decades, and the constant technological acceleration will only continue to ruthlessly drive to extinction those companies that cannot adapt to new circumstances. That's real.

The solution is to change. To adapt and evolve. Scrum is a way of embedding the ability to change into your personal and organizational structure. But be wary of the resistance. Any change, any innovation in a corporation will stimulate the corporate immune system to create antibodies to destroy it.

But why is that? Why do we act that way?

I'm going to give you three examples of times when fear drove people to accept madness as the way things are and to believe it was the only way they could possibly be. In that mindset, questioning that madness is to question the nature of reality itself.

The Madness of Madness

Let me take you inside one of the world's largest automakers. There's a weird thing about large companies, I've found—the farther away you get from actually doing work, the higher your status is, the more money you get, and the fancier your title. Moreover, I find that most of the people who actually do work don't actually work for the company; they work for another company the company hired to actually do the work.

So when this global auto company hires someone to actually work for them as a full-time employee, that person stops doing work. I'm serious. Instead, they are put in charge of managing the people who work for outside contractors. And if you get promoted, you manage the people who manage the work of the people who work for outside contractors or, even better, you manage the managers who manage the managers of people who are doing the work. I know that sounds crazy. It *is* crazy.

At this company, an internal project was being developed to track and deploy sales incentives at their dealerships. This is a relatively straightforward problem. So they put a number of managers on the project. And those managers hired other managers. And those managers hired others. And then the first group, the line managers, hired workers from the outside contractors they deal with for the managers to manage and for the other managers to manage the managers. Eventually there were about two hundred people working on this project. I am not making this up.

They had meetings. Lots of meetings. There were meetings to plan for meetings, and meetings about how many meetings there were. These managers had their days full of important meetings with other important people who made the act of having the meetings with those people a status symbol. After all, if important people attended a meeting, the meeting must be important just because they were present. Everyone who walked past the glass walls of the conference room and saw the really important people meeting would know not only that those people were important but that the meeting must be deciding something really important. And those inside the glass box gained a little bit of joy, and a sense of importance, knowing that other people were experiencing fear because of the very fact that they were watching the more important people meet.

Of course, nothing ever happened. Oh, there were many status reports, and slide decks showing how much work was being done. But it wasn't really work that was getting done. It was people talking about other people doing work. This went on for five years. And nothing was done. Not a single piece of valuable work was completed by these two hundred people for five years. I swear this actually happened.

When I first learned about it I did a little bit of math in my head. Let's be conservative and say the average salary for those people was $75,000. Multiply that by two hundred and you get $15 million a year. Over five years, we're talking at least $75 million—and probably quite a bit more, given the level of managers involved.

So what did they do? They did what people managing these kinds of projects always seem to do—they asked for more people to get this really important project for managing dealer incentives done. If only they had a few more dozen people, they could make this work.

When Scrum Inc. was eventually hired to take a look at this mess (and this was really only a small and, to be honest, not terribly important piece of the greater mess at the company), the first question we asked was, "Who is actually doing the work?" It took our Team a month to figure it out. They spent a lot of that time in meetings being shown slide decks and org charts. When they asked to see the actual work that had been completed, these really important managers and executives were surprised. They wanted to show us the reports about the work rather than the work itself.

Eventually, after many meetings, our Team finally figured out how many people were actually doing the work: twenty-five. And most of them worked for outside contractors.

Our Team advised the automaker to cut 175 people from the project. The endless meetings were only stopped when the Chief Product Owner told the leadership that if they wanted a status report, they could come to a Sprint Review. No more meetings. Or meetings about meetings. And they started to prioritize—picking the right work to do, and in what order. The Teams were able to focus, to drive toward a single goal, Sprint after Sprint. They started showing actual progress every week. Of course, because they were successful, other managers started trying to poach the Team Members for their own projects. But the Chief Product

Owner was able to say no to leadership. *No, you can't have a status report. No, we won't go to those meetings. No, I won't produce a slide deck.* It's the most important word in a Product Owner's vocabulary. If you say yes to everything, nothing will get done.

Those 175 people whose work turned out to be unneeded and unnecessary didn't get fired, of course—they were given other projects to work on. Just months later the twenty-five remaining people on the original Team delivered a working product for the first time in five years.

The weirdest part to me was that before we got there, people would gather in the hallways and have whispered discussions about how absolutely insane the whole thing was, but no one would say it out loud. No one would say the emperor had no clothes. Actually saying so would mean that maybe those managers, and the managers who managed them, weren't totally necessary to the project . . . or maybe to the company.

No One Wants to Work for Us

Scrum Inc. often gets calls from organizations who say they desperately need to change. More and more often recently, those calls have come from large banks, some with assets in the trillions. When you're dealing with big banks, at a certain level it becomes difficult to wrap your head around the sheer magnitude of the numbers.

Let me put that in perspective. The richest man in the world at the moment of this writing is Jeff Bezos. *Forbes* says he was worth $112 billion in 2018. He bought a house in Washington, D.C., the city I live in. The house he bought used to be a museum and it cost him $23 million; it's rumored that he is spending another $20 million on renovations. That seems absurd. But when I did the math, the $43 million Jeff Bezos was spending was equivalent to me spending a couple hundred bucks. A fancy date-night dinner for me was his 27,000-square-foot mansion. That's nation-state kind of money. Jeff Bezos has more money than the GDP of 120 countries. He ranks between Morocco and Kuwait.

Each of the banks I'm talking about has assets an order of magnitude more than that. When I was talking to one of them, I asked, "Why did you call me? You have all the money."

"No one wants to work for us," they replied.

It's not just banks I hear that from. It's insurance companies. It's large industrial companies. It's manufacturers. Often these companies are old behemoths that for decades have faced little competition and had little incentive to change. GE, to give one example, raised entry-level salaries to try to attract more talent. They held public hack-a-thons. They did a slick ad campaign aimed at millennials.

The problem is, when that young talent shows up, they enter a system that just beats them down. They work long hours; they are given no space for creativity; they are micromanaged. Then they talk to their friends at Agile companies and it just sounds like more fun. Young people are highly likely to vote with their feet if they don't like the workplace culture.

Deloitte does an annual survey of millennials across the globe. In a recent one they found that corporate loyalty, measured in terms of whether respondents expect to stay at a place more than two years, has plummeted. A vast majority say they certainly don't expect to be at the same employer in five years. The major factors driving that, aside from pay itself, are a positive workplace culture and flexibility in when, where, and how they work.

All too often the companies say they want to change, they want to be flexible. But when you start explaining what they would have to do to achieve that, they start to say things like, *That's impossible here. This is how things are done here. We've always done it that way. Yes, we want the benefits of Scrum, but we don't want to change our behavior.* It's crazy.

It can be done. You have to actually make things change, though. One hardware manufacturer we work with decided they were going to change the whole place and everyone would be on Scrum Teams. The people who worked there were skeptical. They'd heard this kind of thing before. Empowerment. Getting rid of impediments. Speeding things up by working smarter, not harder.

We were running a two-day Scrum training course for a bunch of their engineers, and by the end of the first day, the new leader of the company knew he had to do something. The engineers just didn't seem to believe it was *possible* to change. So he got up at the beginning of the second day and spoke to the room.

"We need to change the way we work," he said, his voice thick and cracking as he spoke. "Because it sucks. We all know it. It's painful for all of us."

The room was quiet in agreement.

"We all want to do good," he continued. "We want to make the best damn product we can. We want to be proud of what we do."

And then he spoke to the madness they were going to get rid of, starting with the broken toilet in the men's room in the lobby. It had been broken for as long as anyone could remember.

"We've gotten really good at placing tape around the stall," he said. "And really, really good at making signs which read 'Out of Order.'" He paused, thought for a moment, then went on. "Why are we better at that than at fixing the problem? That's a problem in itself. That's why we fixed the toilet."

The crowd was quiet in awe. Seriously. At last one male employee said, "It's about time. Thank you."

Another, a woman from procurement, said, "That's great. But

can you then do something about the sink in the women's room right next door?"

"Yes!" the leader replied. "But only if you all will tell me and your Scrum Masters where the problems are. Otherwise we won't know. We need you to speak up and tell us what is slowing you down."

"Start with that sink, then I'll believe you are serious about this," she replied.

So they did.

You don't have to accept that things are broken and can't be fixed. Even the simple things.

The Clarity of Storms

I had a conversation with a giant U.S. utility in 2017. Their problem, they said, was made crystal clear by the number of times they had to send out a truck to fix a customer's problem. No matter what the problem was—fixing a downed power line, installation of service in a new building, fixing a substation, whatever—usually it took five attempts before the problem was resolved. *Five* crews had to visit one customer for a single problem. Naturally, that results in unhappy customers, but it is also incredibly expensive and wasteful for the utility.

Why did that happen? Well, they'd show up and discover the problem wasn't the problem they were told it was. Or they had been given the wrong address. Or they didn't have the right equipment or the right skills. Or that someone forgot to tell the control center to cut the power so they could work on the lines. The worst part, they said, was when two trucks would pass each other on the same road going in opposite directions to fix the same problem, or would pull up at two houses next door to each other. There was no coordination.

So I asked *why* that was. It turned out that the people who scheduled the trucks worked in a different group than the dispatchers, who were different from the people who put the tools on the trucks, who were different from the people in the control center energizing the cable, who were different from the people actually on the truck. And then there were residential and commercial repair crews, who were in different divisions.

Does this sound familiar? Each of those groups, what are often called functional silos, had to pass things from one group to the next to get anything done for the customer. They weren't all aligned in their interests, their priorities, or their power structure. And they certainly weren't organized around delivering value to the customer. They were organized around internal localized interests. There was a lot of talk there about putting the customer first, as there is everywhere these days, but too often it just doesn't happen.

But then something interesting took place. In the United States there is a storm season, when giant hurricanes whip up from the Caribbean or the South Atlantic, bringing high-velocity winds, deluges of rain, and monstrous storm surges onto the coast in a fury. The worst year since we started keeping track of such hurricanes and tropical storms was 2017; there were seventeen named storms, including ten hurricanes, and six of those were major (category 3 or higher). Hurricanes Maria and Irma devastated the Caribbean islands and lashed Florida. Harvey flooded Galveston and Houston. It was a very bad year.

A hurricane can destroy the communications and power grid—in some cases for weeks, and in the case of Puerto Rico for many, many months. I was at this utility company in the United States a month or so after one of the storms. At one point they'd had hundreds of thousands of customers without power.

They call it "storm time." During storm time, in the frantic effort to restore power to homes and hospitals and cities, all of a sudden all the barriers drop. Utility crews from around the country come together. A VP of marketing might be dishing out scrambled eggs in the morning to keep them fed. The silos disappear. People's lives are at stake, and these people take pride in their work; they deliver come hell or high water.

And after that storm they did. They restored power in a matter of days rather than weeks. It was incredible. But once the damage from the storm was repaired, they looked around at each other, exhausted and triumphant, and went back to work the way they had before, rolling five trucks to fix one problem.

Rules Should Fight for Their Lives

A few years back at NPR, management asked me to go be the line producer of *Morning Edition* for a bit. The line producer is the one who decides what goes in the show, in what order, and for how long. It was fun. Having to be there at midnight wasn't particularly enjoyable, but the work was fun.

One day—I forget what the news was—I wanted to put two interviews together, followed by a piece. Elections, military news, congressional shenanigans. Whatever it was. Anyway, I put that on the board, and one of the producers who had been on the show for years said, "You can't do that."

"What?"

"You can't put two interviews back to back."

"Why?"

"It's a rule."

"That's a stupid rule."

"It's about the texture of the show, J.J. You're just a fill-in—you probably don't understand how we think about the sound and texture of *Morning Edition*."

"Really?"

"Here, let me show you."

And he pulled down a white three-ring binder that was labeled "How We Do *Morning Edition*" or some such nonsense. Sure enough, the manual said I couldn't do what I wanted to do. So I caved, for the moment.

I spent the next three days tracking down who had written that rule. I wanted to have a word. Eventually I got Jay Kernis on the phone. He was the person who launched *Morning Edition* back in 1978.

"Jay, I've got a question about this rule."

"Which one?"

"The one that says I can't do a whole bunch of the same thing in a row."

"Oh, that was because the reel-to-reel machines couldn't rewind fast enough, so we had to space the recorded stuff out."

I'd like to point out that while there were still reel-to-reel tape machines in the control room, they were there because they were heavy and no one had thrown them out yet. We'd been using a digital audio system for years at this point.

I tell you that story because I am pretty sure that you too have a few of those rules in your organization. There are always some. One company I know of was taking three to six months to update copy on their website because once, years ago, something was put up that they were fined for by the regulators in their industry. And so everything, whether it needed to be or not, was now reviewed by this small compliance group. It was the head of compliance who called me: his Team was the roadblock and he couldn't seem to get around this rule. I asked him how much of the stuff he reviewed actually even touched a regulatory area. Maybe 10 percent, he told me. *How about this?* I said. *Before the Teams start writing, why don't you sit down and walk through their backlogs and flag the items that are poten-*

tially dangerous, and explain what they need to be sure to do for those particular pieces of copy? After that small change, they were able to update the site daily. Something that simple changed what was possible for them to do.

Now, it's not that the people who made that rule were stupid or ill-intentioned. Both of those rules existed for a very good reason *at the time they were implemented*. But things change. Technology changes. Regulations change. The environment changes. I often refer to those kinds of rules as "organizational scar tissue." If a rule seems dumb, it might actually be dumb and you should figure out who can change it. Someone can. It's not natural law.

The Sarbanes-Oxley Act was signed into law in 2002, soon after the disastrous scandals at Enron, WorldCom, and Tyco International. And SOX, as it is known, has some teeth: if a CEO or CFO knowingly submits false data to a SOX compliance audit, they can face a fine of up to $5 million and up to twenty years in jail. It is not kidding around. Every single public company and international company registered with the U.S. Securities and Exchange Commission, and any accounting firm that provides services to such a company, has to be SOX compliant.

Every year all of those companies have to hire an outside auditor to audit their finances and their internal controls. The audit looks at access to financial data, security, change management, and how their data is backed up. It's pretty thorough.

My colleague Kim Antelo was working at a large global industrial company a few years back. They make things that keep airplanes in the sky. Important stuff. Her group was totally Scrum, and without letting her know, the SOX compliance group audited them. The auditors pulled her into a meeting and said she had failed horribly: the Team wasn't doing this and that, she needed to put in all these controls, she didn't have voluminous Business Requirement Documents (BRDs).

"You're right," she said. "I don't have those things. But I can prove we are actually doing more of what you are asking us to do in a much more efficient way."

Turns out Sarbanes-Oxley doesn't actually state how you have to prove you have the correct internal controls; it only specifies that you have to have some way to prove that you do. She asked them to take a step back and look at the spirit of the controls and why they exist. Then she walked them through how her group was meeting them.

"We don't have the BRD you're looking for, true, but we have a Product Owner who is pulling things into a Sprint every two weeks. They've signed off on the requirements. You can see in our Product Backlog tool who wrote the code. Who peer-reviewed it. Who submitted the merge request. Who approved the merge request. You can see all the tests. You can see all the documentation." She pointed out that Scrum is more transparent and provides more data about what is happening and has happened than traditional audits ask for.

"You're right," said the auditor. "This Agile process is a much better way."

She thought that was the end of it. Then the CIO of the entire humongous conglomerate asked her to lead a session for leaders across the company to show them how to do it.

"The old rules don't apply anymore," he said to the group. "What do we need to do to make things better?"

Listen, I know there are some rules you can't do anything about. Maybe corporate policy is common across all business units and you simply can't change it. I get it. But at least test the boundaries a bit. See if what you think is immovable actually has a little give once you push on it.

Just one more example. Many years ago at Siemens they were drowning in the number of documents and reports they had to produce. And no one, quite literally no one, had the authority to change them. So, as an experiment the Teams started putting garbage text on a page in the middle of the document with a phone number to call if anyone had trouble reading it. If no one called for six weeks, they stopped producing that particular document or report. The rules said they had to do it, and they mindlessly followed them. The rules were in charge, not the people. That is so crazy it verges on Kafkaesque. Make every rule fight for its life occasionally. The people deserve it.

Things That Seem Crazy Usually Are

All of the scenarios I've mentioned in this chapter are, not to be too on the nose, just crazy. The craziest part to me is that the people involved in these situations get so acclimated to the crazy they can no longer see just how crazy they are. They are also, sadly, all too common. I'm sure they seem crazy to you too. But I would bet good money that if we walked through the way things work in your company or organization, we would find plenty of things just as redolent of this kind of madness. A tip-off is if you find yourself saying things like:

"That's just the way things work around here."

"That will never change."

"I know it seems crazy, but . . ."

When people and places seem out of whack, the vast majority of the time they are. Human beings are miracles of adaptation and justification. It's how we survive. It's what we do. We find ourselves in impossible situations and make whatever mental adjustments are needed to survive. And let me reassure you, it isn't just you. The people at the bottom of the hierarchy are no different from the people at the top. We all get trapped in this. What we need to do is put guardrails around Teams, tell them the purpose of those rules, the meaning, the reason they exist, and empower them to challenge the rules if they don't make sense anymore and don't actually deliver what they were intended to do.

Do you think the people at the top with too much work to do and too little time to do it wanted it to be that way? They told themselves they were just acting in accordance with the forces being applied to them. It's the same at a bank as it is at a power company as it is at an industrial giant. The people whom everyone expects to be able to fix the problem are just as much products of the system as everyone else. They often see themselves as subject to the whims of fate, precisely because they are aware of the multitude of pressures being put on them.

In recovery from addiction, they say the first step is admitting you have a problem. That may be true, but in the business world, usually the people I talk to are well aware that they have a problem. That they can't get things done. That they have a toxic or broken or imperfect workplace. That unless things change, things will get worse.

To me, the first step is saying, *Sure, I have a problem, but I can fix it. I can change the situation I am in. I can do something different. It doesn't have to be this way.*

And it doesn't. Even big organizations can change, and quickly.

Why? Because organizations, like people, are emergent phenomena of complex adaptive systems. You cannot understand the whole by understanding the parts. Unsurprisingly, it's the same from the individual to the mass level. We are products not of individual parts of a system, but of the interrelationship of those parts.

At the individual level, it's the difference between the brain and the mind or consciousness. There is no one piece of your brain where "you" resides. "You" does not sit in the frontal cortex and make requests from all the other parts of the brain. No one part of the brain conducts all the other parts when you need to say something or solve the quite complicated physics calculations needed to catch a ball. No, all those systems are connected in complex and often irritating ways, and "you" exists as a product of all of those parts in relationship with each other. It emerges from your many different selves. "You," in any real sense of the word, balances on a knife edge of neurons and the electricity that binds the body and brain together. Overwhelm either, or change the electrical flow, and who you are changes. It can happen with a whack in the head, from exercising, from deep meditation, from falling in love, from being afraid, or from having one too many once too often.

Every single day, you are a different person when you wake up. All those different parts of your brain test the connections and weigh the flow. None of them are intelligent in any way it can be defined. But the result of those connections is greater than the sum of the parts. And so "you" emerges from sleep. The idea that your identity is continuous is an illusion. We believe it, though, because acknowledging we aren't continuous is, well, uncomfortable, to say the least.

The same is true of any organization. All these different individuals come together every day, and through their relationships with each other, they decide what the organization will be that day. They adhere to some set of rules about how to talk to each other and how to make decisions. And every single day the organization is created anew. It's a decision, not an inevitability.

Why Can't It Be Storm Time All the Time?

Dr. Otto Scharmer, a professor at MIT's Sloan School of Management, has a theory. It's that everyone's afraid. We are driven by fear. And fear controls us.

As any number of studies have shown, people who are afraid are not very creative. They tend to fall back on old patterns, what Scharmer calls downloading. When working in a world of rapid change we cannot understand, we download past behaviors, even if they are demonstrably ineffective, or even countereffective, in the current environment. And yet we defend these behaviors to the death. We lay down barricades and say *no más*. If we cannot control the way the world is changing, at least we can control the degree to which we change. And thus we condemn ourselves to the proverbial dustbin of history.

Scharmer says that to move beyond this fear, we have to move past three voices that are part of our inner dialogue.

Voice of Judgment

The first is the Voice of Judgment—judging new information through our existing worldview. Actual facts or data don't sway us; what we really want is confirmation of what we already believe. Political scientists see this in research on the polarized political dynamic currently at play in many parts of the world. No matter what events or actions take place, they are viewed through the lens of partisan identity. Everything that is said and done only reinforces our previously held positions. There are only two sides to any position, our side and the wrong side. The world becomes monochromatic.

This kind of confirmation bias, or lack of ability to think critically, happens to all of us in some aspects of our lives. The trick here is to realize it is happening—not only to the people you are so strongly in opposition to, but to yourself as well. If you are a leader in an organization, you have to recognize that this is happening inside your company as well. It can limit your organization's ability to grow and change, even what your organization is able to consider. It can actively fight the change you are trying to implement.

Simply acknowledging that it takes place can be a powerful tool in getting beyond it. Often our fear is driven by something that people are trying to protect. At one company I worked with, they have a legendary reputation for engineering of the highest caliber. When we tried to introduce Scrum, the greatest resistance came from middle managers, who embodied this Voice of Judgment. They worked feverishly to resist change, maneuvering behind senior management's back to sabotage the transformation the company was trying to achieve. They would say yes in a meeting but find ways to resist and derail whatever the initiative was.

At first, my reaction was probably a mirror of their reaction to me: they were backstabbing idiots. But no matter how rewarding it might feel to look down on people, it solves nothing. Even if you're right. Which I was. They were dinosaurs. They were going to kill this company, and only I could save it.

Of course, in reality, I was completely wrong. They were protecting what they had devoted their professional lives to. Middle management owns the culture of a company. They embody it. They saw Scrum as threatening that culture, threatening their livelihood and their company. They had helped to create and sustain a culture of excellence that they were proud of. So I had to show them—*convince* them—not that they had to change their ideals but that this new way of working would enhance them. I had to prove that they could actually achieve better quality faster. That Scrum would allow them to experience more fully what they felt so strongly.

Voice of Cynicism

Scharmer's second voice is the Voice of Cynicism. Listen, I was a journalist for twenty years. Cynicism was my stock in trade. I covered the military in wartime; cynicism was the most appropriate response the vast majority of the time. Distrust of the untruths that are being fed us is a healthy thing. You want that in journalists.

To an organization, though, cynicism is death. That said, cynicism in a company that is struggling is totally understandable. Management will say one thing but do another. Or they will implement another fad, another ill-considered reorganization, another so-called silver bullet that makes them feel better but makes most employees' jobs worse.

There's this one company, a big company—one of the most-recognized brands on the planet. And like most large organizations, they are facing a rapidly changing world and are finding they simply can't get stuff done. Everyone is busy, but they can't bring new products to the market, to done. Competitors are starting to eat up their market share. New innovators won't agree to let themselves be bought. The company is missing the boat on whole new categories. And for the start-ups they do buy, they seem to inevitably destroy the rationale that they bought them for in the first place.

About a year ago, the CEO decided they were going to become Agile. The whole company. They would empower their people. They would devolve decision-making down to the teams themselves, the people closest to the market. They would embrace innovation, a culture of failing fast, learning quickly, and celebrating it. They were going to break down silos! The CEO even put that in their annual report. He was deadly serious.

Or it seemed so, until you talked to the people a few layers down the food chain. They told me cynically that it didn't matter what the CEO said. The middle managers just wouldn't do it. They wouldn't let teams make decisions for themselves, or break down silos, or do any of the other things Agile is designed to do. This wasn't the first time they'd attended the training sessions and gone to the town halls and gotten the follow-up emails. Nothing had changed before, so why should they believe this time would be different?

What cynicism does is to protect you emotionally from feeling hope only to have it shattered later. It distances you from what is happening. It allows you to avoid feeling the pain when it doesn't work out. It's a natural instinct. But it also destroys initiative and ruins marriages and companies alike. It is a survival mechanism that leads to emotional betrayal.

So here's what I told them to do. *Print out the CEO's statement*, I said. *And when a manager or program director or whoever stops you from getting things done solely through resistance to change—by holding on to power, or by insisting on working on fifteen top priorities—show it to them. Ask them if the CEO is a liar. And if they insist anyway, go to their boss, and theirs, until, if necessary, you get to the CEO's office and ask him the question. But I don't think you will have to go that far. Because if the CEO is serious and you call a manager out on their refusal to embrace the new program, you'll find that corrective action will be taken on the next level up, or the level after that. And if not, then you know that the company isn't actually serious about it.*

Amazingly enough, it worked. Slowly, to be sure. They're not done. But Team by Team, location by location, one Sprint at a time, they are actually driving real change through their company. It takes discipline. It takes focus. It takes commitment. But it can be done.

Voice of Fear

The last voice to deal with, in Scharmer's taxonomy, is the Voice of Fear, where I started this chapter. Think about your job right now, your most important project. Let me just whisper a few questions in your ear. *What if I fail? What will my boss think of me? What will my Team think of me? What will my family think of me if I'm fired? What will my father think of me?*

That's fear. That's real fear.

And it lives within all of us, in that little amygdala nestled so comfortably in the center of our brain, all too ready to insist we abandon all conscious thought and just run or fight. That's the fear that shocks us awake in the middle of the night.

But if we want to create something new, if we want to help guide others into undiscovered territory, if we want to have a great team or a great company, we have to acknowledge the fear and let it go. We have to be comfortable with uncertainty and change, with making decisions on incomplete information. At seeing a future in the mist and saying to others, *I see it—it's real. We can get there together.*

W. Edwards Deming was the man who taught the Japanese the entire concept of continuous improvement after World War II. In later years he became deeply concerned with the state of American business. Deming eventually published a book in the 1980s called *Out of the Crisis*, because he saw American industry at the time facing an existential crisis similar to Japan's postwar situation. He developed a list of fourteen things companies should do, such as "Improve constantly and forever" and "Institute leadership." I want to particularly look at number 8: "Drive out fear."

Where there is fear, said Deming, there will be wrong numbers. Or as Peter Drucker put it: "Modern behavioral psychology has demonstrated that great fear coerces, while remnants of fear cause only resentment and resistance. . . . Lesser fears destroy motivation."[1]

I could quote many others about psychological safety, trust, and the building of great organizations. But the real thing is that fear is a mind-killer. For yourself, for your team, and for your organization.

And that's why it isn't "storm time" all the time. People are afraid to make the changes they need to make. They are afraid of the disruption that is fracturing their industry—and the planet. It is a perfectly rational fear, to be honest. But it will keep you and your organization trapped in a cycle of denial and reprisal, treating people like replaceable cogs, customers like enemies, and colleagues like backstabbing courtiers.

That is a truly dreary way to live.

But you don't have to, you know. You can wake up tomorrow and decide to be something different.

People Are Connection

I had lunch recently with Professor Ikujiro Nonaka of Hitotsubashi University, the leading business school in Japan. Nonaka is the coauthor of the paper that coined the term *Scrum* back in 1986. He said the key to building a great organization, and the mission of great leaders, is to create the environment where innovation happens. And that that environment exists in the connection between people. He used the Japanese word *ba*, which translates loosely as "a context that harbors meaning." It's a shared space between individuals that is the foundation for knowledge creation.

Nonaka used the metaphor of points of view. When we speak of ourselves, we talk in the first person: *I did this, I felt that, I am this*—the ego, to use the Freudian metaphor of mind. When we talk about organizations or groups, we talk in the third person: *they did this, this place is this way, this company acts like that*. And if we leave it there, if we see the world as atomized and separate at the individual level and as "other" and "not us" at the organizational level, that's when things go bad. We see every interaction as a transaction. We talk about a dog-eat-dog world. We see those who disagree with us as servants of an evil ideology because they are threatening our day-to-day existence. It is a zero-sum game: I win, you lose, and anyone who doesn't view the world that way is a sucker. It's a philosophy of selfishness and scarcity.

Nonaka said that what creates the space for innovation to happen, for creation to happen, is moving from "I" and "they" to "we." He said that humanity exists in that connection. The Japanese kanji character for "humanity" is an ideogram of two people facing each other. Humanity itself exists only in the connection between people. When you are in a partnership, or participating on a team, or working together, or having hundreds of teams aligned on a single goal, you create something larger than the sum of the parts. It has an identity, a personality, a life of its own. It's why we celebrate them coming together and mourn them when they fall apart. It's why *widow* and *orphan* are among our saddest words, and *family* and *marriage* and *birth* among our happiest. It's why we are excited at the beginnings of projects and grieve when they are over and the team says goodbye after the storm passes. It's why breakups are hard and getting the band back together is one of our greatest joys. We exist only in relationship.

At Scrum Inc., we are scattered all over the world. As of this writing we have Teams in Japan, Germany, Texas, Massachusetts, the United Kingdom, Australia, Singapore, and Mexico. We work globally. Every quarter we all stop work and fly into one city and meet up physically. We talk. We have fun. We break bread together. Not much work gets done, to be totally honest. We do it to maintain connection with each other. To keep our *ba* strong. I can usually tell just how long it has been since we have done that by looking at the frequency of flame wars that erupt in Slack. They start breaking out about ten weeks after we've last had a gathering. It's almost like clockwork. Getting together this way is expensive, both in cash and in opportunity cost. But that investment pays off with a much happier and more aligned Team. It's totally worth it.

It is a leader's job to make sure those relationships are healthy. That the community is strong. That there is a fertile ground for problem-solving, creativity, and innovation. That's the antidote to fear: connection.

THE TAKEAWAY

Recognize crazy for what it is. People involved in crazy situations get so acclimated to the crazy they can no longer see just how crazy they are. Which is why you often hear people say things like "That's just the way things work around here," or "That will never change," or "I know it seems crazy, but . . ." Fighting against crazy is a zero-sum game. If crazy wins, you lose.

Rules should fight for their lives. Rules were created for a very good reason *at the time they were implemented*. But things change. Technology changes. The environment changes. If a rule seems dumb, it might actually be dumb, and you should figure out who can change it. Someone can. It's not natural law.

Make it "storm time." You have the ability to work in a deliberate, focused way—all the time. People are afraid to make the changes they need to make. It is a perfectly rational fear, to be honest. But it will keep you and your organization trapped in a cycle of denial and reprisal. You can wake up tomorrow and decide to be something different.

Find your ba. It's a shared space between individuals that is the foundation for knowledge creation. When you are in a partnership or participating on a team or teams aligned on a single goal, you create something larger than the sum of the parts. And it is a leader's job to make sure those relationships are healthy. That the community is strong. That there is a fertile ground for problem-solving, creativity, and innovation. That's the antidote to fear: connection.

BACKLOG

- Think about each of the voices in Otto Scharmer's taxonomy of fear:

    - *Voice of Judgment.* When we judge new information through our existing worldview, actual facts or data don't sway us—what we really want is confirmation of what we already believe.

    - *Voice of Cynicism.* Some cynicism can be good, but too much can be the death of an organization. The cynic is always against the new. Whether changes are good or bad, the cynic sees them as nothing more than a placebo that will make others feel better but make the cynic's job worse.

    - *Voice of Fear.* Think about your job right now, your most important project. Let me just whisper a few questions in your ear: *What if I fail? What will my boss think of me? What will my team think of me? What will my family think of me if I'm fired?*

  Which voice (or voices) best describes you and how you think? What can you do to remedy that?

- What rules or situations have you accepted as normal, even though they were actually crazy? Which have you fought? Why is the former list longer than the latter?

- How connected are you to the people you work with? Do something to increase that connection.

CHAPTER 6

Structure Is Culture

Riccardo's is a small, local place in the Chelsea neighborhood in London. "A Taste of Tuscany" is written in white on the red awning under the name. And the menu is full of Tuscan classics: pappa al pomodoro, ribollita, pappardelle con ragú di cervo, and the like. Riccardo Mariti opened the place in 1995. His father was from Tuscany, and Riccardo had fond memories of the food at his grandmother's table when he went to visit as a child. The restaurant seats ninety, with space for forty to fifty more outside when the weather allows. On a good night they turn the tables two, maybe three times.

A couple of years ago, Riccardo came to a conclusion. The way his restaurant was being managed just wasn't going to work anymore. Restaurants, he told me, are heavily hierarchical, perhaps the worst workplaces to have the misfortune to be in. Managers and chefs abuse their team members and don't allow them to think for themselves. He actually thought about leaving the business entirely. Selling the place.

Then he discovered Scrum, starting with my first book. Then he began to attend Scrum Inc. training sessions, one after the other: first in Germany, then Sweden, then Boston. Then he went back to his restaurant and changed everything.

"In Scrum," he says, "no one tells you what to do. They tell you what needs to be done, but you figure out the best way of doing it. And, you know, that really resonated with me."

He went back and told his staff they needed a new operating system. A new way of running the restaurant. *All of you have job security,* he said, *but no one has role security.* No more managers. Everyone was now a Team Member, including him.

He offered them a share in the profits. Some took him up on it. Some didn't. But the hierarchy had completely changed, from an autocracy to a totally flat organization. No titles. No bosses. Just people figuring out together how to serve customers better, faster, and happier.

What Riccardo figured out is that your structure is your culture. And your culture defines your limits. A rigid structure begets a rigid cultural and product architecture. It makes change dramatically more difficult. That's true at the Team level, but it's even truer and more important at the organizational level.

Your structure is more than just your org chart. One of my mentors, Darrell Rigby of Bain & Company, told me once that two companies can have very similar org charts but very, very different cultures and operating models.

"I find it easier to talk about operating models as a broad context for how an org works," he says. "That's a combination of 'What is our purpose and our passion?,' 'How do our leaders behave?,' 'What is our culture like?,' 'What are our strategic systems?,' 'How does budgeting work?,' and 'What kind of people do we hire?' Org charts are just one of many elements that make up that operating model."

He compares the org chart to the hardware of the company. It's important, but even more important is the software that runs on it, that operating model. And to my mind you have to change both to get real results.

So your structure is more than just your org chart. It's your values. It's what you reward. It's what outcomes you organize your Teams around. Out of those emerges your culture. You can't decide what it is, but you must enable its creation. To build a generative company, you need the bones.

Human Constraints

There are things that no matter how much we wish they weren't true, are. They seem to be baked into human nature so deeply they are impossible to avoid when you bring people together to accomplish anything. And you should be aware of them. The first is what is known as Conway's law, so named because Melvin Conway coined the idea in a paper titled "How Do Committees Invent" back in 1968. "Organizations which design systems (in the broad sense used here)," he wrote, "are constrained to produce designs which are copies of the communication structures of these organizations."[1]

The year 1968, by the way, is the same year they introduced Hot Wheels, the beanbag chair, and Ziploc bags. And like them, Conway's law has stood the test of time. Researchers at MIT, Harvard Business School, the University of Maryland, and even Microsoft itself have found it to be true over and over again.

The second thing you need to be aware of is Shalloway's corollary, first coined a few years back by Al Shalloway, CEO of Net Objectives and a longtime thinker on these topics: "When development groups change how their development staff are organized, their current application architecture will work against them."

Let's consider those two ideas for a bit. Conway's law basically states that whatever you are making or doing, be it software, cars, rocket ships, restaurants, whatever, your product or service will reflect in its architecture, in how the pieces are put together, a replica of your communication patterns. If you have a rigid, hierarchical organization that is difficult, is resistant to change, hides information, and communicates slowly if at all, you will have a product that is hierarchical, rigid, difficult, and resistant to change. Hard to maintain. Hard to upgrade. Hard to adapt to new realities or new forces.

Again, this may or may not be reflected in your org chart. You can set up cross-functional Scrum Teams across functional silos. And in the beginning that may be all you can do. Your communication structure can be different from your organizational structure. Over time, you will want to change your organizational structure to reflect your communication pathways, otherwise they will fight with each other. But it is far better to let that new structure emerge as the work is being done.

Just like when you are making a product, you don't know what the right structure is going to be when you begin. That's the real arrogance of waterfall. Failing to recognize that you just don't know. Part of being Agile is making the confession that you don't know the answers and you can't predict the future; the right solution will emerge from doing the work, getting feedback, and iterating toward the best solution at the time.

There isn't any "correct" structure. A defense contractor, a big bank, and a billion-dollar online gaming company will be different. They are doing very, very different things. They have different goals and different strategies. The right structure for each will also be very, very different.

Let me give you an example. Jacob Sisk is an old friend. He's the CEO of an innovation lab for a global financial institution.

They're the moonshot guys for one of the biggest banks on the planet. A few years back, he and I met up in Amsterdam. He was living in Zurich and I was in the Netherlands on business.

It was a cloudy afternoon when he and I meandered through the velvet green of the Vondelpark and made our way to one of the world's great museums, the Rijksmuseum. Its collection of Dutch masters—Rembrandt, Vermeer, and others—is astounding. If you haven't ever seen Rembrandt's grand masterpiece *The Night Watch*, which depicts a Dutch militia company setting out on patrol, it truly is worth a visit. As you walk up the stairs to where it grandly dominates the space, the first thing you notice is its sheer size. The painting is simply gigantic, twelve feet high and fourteen across. Its composition and light make it feel like the subjects might march right out of the wall to the beat of their drummer boy.

As we looked at it, Jacob told me a very interesting story about the museum we were in. For well over a hundred years the collection's display exactly replicated the museum's organization. Each department—paintings, sculpture, ceramics, what have you—was incredibly siloed, not only in its reporting structure but also in the very physical layout of the displays themselves. If you were interested in paintings, you began in the 1200s, then moved through time, obviously stopping for quite a while at the seventeenth-century Dutch Golden Age, and then moving year by year, decade by decade, to the present. In the next hall—say, sculpture—you would begin again in the medieval period and move through history. Then you'd start again in ceramics. The museum's exhibit halls were a direct copy of its org chart.

In 2003 the museum closed for a decade-long restoration. Planning its grand reopening in 2013, the director of collections at the time, Taco Dibbits, decided to do something different. He decided to organize the museum by century, so visitors could get a sense of the art of a period, not just a particular type of art. Artists exist contemporaneously: they are influenced by each other, go to each other's openings, argue about the nature of aesthetics and the purpose of art. If you separate them by medium, you can't see that conversation in their work.

To do this, the museum had to form cross-functional teams made up of specialists. This was a major change. Before this, the different groups of curators barely interacted with each other. Now they had to work together to select which pieces, from the museum's collection of about a million, would be shown together. In all, they could pick only eight thousand. Each century had a team.

The Rijksmuseum reopened to much fanfare, the restoration was hailed as a resounding success. The *Guardian* said of it at the time: "The long-awaited results are so spectacular that the museum looks likely to prove a model to other institutions for years to come." But the effort left the museum staff exhausted. Dibbits said it was time to ask themselves, *Now that we've done this, what can we do? How do we remain relevant?* They created new Agile cross-functional teams, including everyone from curators to security guards, to really think about how people experience the museum and individual exhibitions. The structure determined what they were now capable of. They didn't go completely Scrum—they had legacy structures—but for their important problems, and for the overarching goal of maintaining relevancy in a rapidly changing world, the structure had to be broken down, because it was limiting what was possible for them to do.

When I told that story to Darrell Rigby, he immediately asked, "How did they know that organizing by era was better than by category?" He pointed out the really interesting question is how you create experiences that customers will find most valuable and most beneficial. He gets that question all the time when he works with large department stores. Most of them are organized by brand, you know—the Under Armour gym over here, and the Body Shop warm wood shack next door looking completely different. But there are "always people who argue that that's not the way to set up a department store," he says, who argue that the store should be set up by category. "They go back and forth all the time."

The real question, he says, is how you get close enough to the customer to figure out what is best for them. At the Rijksmuseum their teams include all the roles in the museum, especially those who interact with visitors—the security guards, the docents, the ticket takers, the shop workers—as well as the curators. And they work together, across organizational silos, to create a whole experience for visitors. They are constantly iterating: *How do we get better? How are customers changing in their habits? How can we meet people where they are?*

At Adobe, after they moved to Scrum more than a decade ago, the Teams decided they needed more customer feedback to do exactly this. Before Scrum, the only customer input they had were bug reports. As a result, they weren't making the things that customers wanted. So they decided to change that. The Flash Pro Team invited super-users to each Sprint Review. Other Teams set up private servers and gave access to their most passionate customers. They got closer and closer to the customer. Now, I'm told, they no longer build features no one is going to use, which is something they used to do. Often.

Management Becomes Leadership

A common mistake management makes when transitioning to a Scrum organization is to think their jobs won't change. They want to get all the benefits of Scrum, more value delivered radically more quickly with higher quality, but they don't realize they have to change their behavior as well.

At Riccardo's restaurant, when they got rid of all the managerial roles, it wasn't just the behavior of the staff that had to change. Riccardo had to change his own behavior as well. He had to not interfere. It's not easy.

"I'm impulsive and love solving problems," he said one day, sitting among the red chairs and walls that define the place. "My default when someone brings me a problem was to solve it." He had to unlearn that behavior. Now, he says, he isn't a decision-maker; he helps them make better decisions. And he had to encourage his staff to make their own decisions. That was a tough change for people who were so used to the strict hierarchies of the restaurant world. People kept looking to Product Owners or Scrum Masters and waiting to be told what to do.

"What we've done," he said one day, standing in front of a Scrum board in his restaurant, the noise of dishwashers occasionally drowning him out, "is tell every Team Member they have to make the decision themselves."

Pushing those decisions down onto the Team has had a dramatic impact. The amount of time it takes to respond to a customer issue has dropped 70 percent. They make those decisions and resolve the issue *three times faster*. But to do that, management has to step back and shift their role from management to leadership.

In an Agile company, leadership is even more necessary than in a formally structured company. With a traditional org chart, it can take forever for an executive's orders to drift down through the organization; they wind up being reinterpreted at each level, and often eventually produce things that no one wanted in the first place, like in the Adobe case. The game of corporate telephone birthed a cuckoo product. In a way, that slowness is an organizational defense mechanism; it gives you a buffer, a delay between a bad call and bad consequences. Not that the bad consequences won't show up, but there is a chance—not a great one, but it is there—that your bad idea will be fixed before it becomes reality.

One day shortly after becoming CEO of his lab, Jacob told me he had realized something that terrified him: the distance between his bad decision and the pain its impact causes is zero. There is no buffer. With a seemingly casual decision he can cripple his organization. I told him that was great! Now he'd get feedback on the impact of his bad decisions every Sprint. With Scrum, you can always change your mind.

The First Thing a Leader Needs to Do Is Lead

Leaders need to have a compelling vision, a compelling direction, a way forward into the undiscovered country, and they need to communicate that out to their people. They need their people to be excited about what they are doing, whether it's changing the world, delivering a better product in a new way that will disrupt the market, or simply getting their great ideas out the door faster than they ever could before.

But be wary of falling too much in love with your beautiful, compelling vision of what your customers want. Just like with everything else, you will be wrong more often than not. There is often the assumption that when an innovation fails, it's because the original specifications were wrong and the Teams weren't able to adapt. We know that original specs are wrong two-thirds of the time. Your compelling vision is probably wrong with about the same frequency.

You have to create an environment that encourages creativity, risk-taking, and swift execution. And it's important to have a tight feedback loop to let you know if your vision or your product or service or idea is actually worth doing. One multibillion-dollar videogame company I know of—it has two thousand employees, and I would bet hard cash you have played their games whether you consider yourself a gamer or not—does this ruthlessly. If someone has an idea for a new game, they'll put it on the backlog of one of their Teams as their top priority. Within a month, they have built a minimum viable product of the game, put it in the marketplace, gauged market reaction and possible growth, and decided whether to kill it or invest more time in adding to it. Killing a game—deciding what *not* to do, finding out that the vision was wrong—is seen as critically valuable.

You have to set up incentives in a way that's often completely opposite from how an org chart operates. In a traditional organization the rewards are set up to incentivize tribalism and self-interest. Instead, you have to reward behaviors that you want and simply not tolerate those you don't. You have to have a set of values that you embody, encourage, and celebrate.

An Unfortunate Peculiarity of the Human Psyche

We are all liars. We all lie. But not all of us lie all the time. There is some fascinating research showing that most adults don't tell that many lies. The number you often hear is that on average people tell one to two lies a day. But remember, that's the average. The distribution of lies is interesting: about half the lies are told by 5 percent of the people. Sixty percent of people don't report telling any lies at all in any particular twenty-four-hour period.

But that's the average day. In certain situations, almost all of us lie. In job interviews, one study showed that 90 percent of people lie. It might not be an outright lie—maybe it's just a shading of the truth here and there—but there is a conscious attempt at deception. Adolescents, that pack of liars, 82 percent say they've lied to their parents on at least one of six topics: money, alcohol and drugs, friends, dating, parties, and sex. Infidelity? Whew, do cheaters lie—it's kinda the whole thing. Ninety-two percent of us, when asked anonymously, report lying to a current or past sexual partner. And I kinda figure that the other 8 percent are lying about their lying.

Here's the thing about lying: the very act of telling a lie changes us. Our neurochemistry shifts with every deceit. A few scientists from Duke University and University College London decided to find out what happens inside our brains when we lie. They put people into an fMRI machine and had them play a game where they lied to their partner. The first time people told a lie, our old friend the amygdala weighed in. It released chemicals that give us that familiar fear, that sinking sense of guilt we get when we lie.

But then the researchers went one step further. They rewarded people for lying. They gave them a small monetary reward for deceiving their partner without them knowing they'd been lied to. Once people started getting rewarded for lying and not getting caught, that amygdala-driven sense of guilt started to fade. Interestingly, it faded most markedly when the lie would hurt someone else but help the person telling it. So people started telling more and more outlandish lies—the whole "slippery slope" thing.

The researchers summed up their findings in a paper called "The Brain Adapts to Dishonesty," and concluded:

> The results show the possible dangers of regular engagement in small acts of dishonesty, perils that are frequently observed in domains ranging from business to politics and law enforcement. These insights can have implications for policy makers in designing deterrents to halt deceit. Despite being small at the outset, engagement in dishonest acts may trigger a process that leads to larger acts of dishonesty further down the line.[2]

It's the classic story of how temptation leads us down the garden path, this time written in brain chemistry. The governors evolution put into place to keep us from lying start getting turned off bit by bit. Ended by repetition. An honest person slowly turns themselves into a fundamentally dishonest person by, quite literally, altering their mind.

That's a touch disturbing, no? I assume you are now running through all the lies you've recently told and wondering if you too have crossed some sort of threshold, doing something you'd never thought you would do even though you know it is hurting someone else. That's a pretty depressing part of human nature.

But it's also a great part of human nature, because it's really easy to change. And you do that by not rewarding lying. You reward other behaviors instead. You reward a moral code. In Scrum we lay this out in the five Scrum values. And if you want to be a leader, you need to make sure behaving in these ways is rewarded, not deception.

The Scrum Values

Over the course of years of developing Scrum, it came to be clear that an open, transparent, and effective organization requires certain values. There are five of them, and like the individual elements of the framework itself, they interlock and build on each other. In a way, they are the lifeblood of Scrum; all the other pieces, the events and artifacts, are empty without it.

You can tell when you walk in the door of a company that's a great place to work. There is an energy, a feeling that people want to come to work. All of these values need to be in place to make a great company that's a fun place to be and dedicated to making great things happen.

Commitment

Each person on a Scrum Team has to be committed—to each other, to the change they are trying to make, to the work they have all said they will complete each Sprint, to producing something of value. This is not simply saying *We will try to do this, we will try to complete the work, we will try to do Scrum.* It is saying *We will do our absolute best to do so.*

Change is hard, and without commitment you simply can't do it. But people being committed to making a real change in their lives is the first step. People need to commit to constantly seeking to be better—better people, better Teams, and better, more successful companies for their customers and the people who work there.

One of the strongest motivators in the human psyche is doing valuable work well. People feel fulfilled when they are creating something of value. In Scrum, the commitment to constantly trying to do that is critical. Without that nothing matters.

Often people will say that commitment asks too much. Instead, they say, they'll try. But trying without commitment means you certainly aren't going to win the World Cup or the Super Bowl. You won't reach greatness without the people on your Teams being committed to a goal.

Without commitment, none of the other values matter, Scrum doesn't matter. It all begins with people committing to themselves and to each other. Work should be fast, easy, and fun. If you're not having fun, you're doing it wrong. But it requires working—and thinking—in a different way.

Committing to each other to get the work done is palpable at Riccardo's restaurant. One of the big changes they've made, even as they've expanded into multiple restaurants, is that everyone agrees that they are all working together to serve the customer. "So what we now do is all Team Members have to subordinate whatever they're doing when the restaurant is busy," says Riccardo. Joe might be working in the marketing department during the day, but if the front of the house calls up and says it looks like they're going to get busy, he drops whatever he is doing and runs upstairs to clean dishes or clear tables. It doesn't happen every day. But when it does, the waiters and line cooks and bussers all know the rest of the Team is with them. They've committed to it.

I wish it was like that all the time. But it requires focus.

Focus

After the Team commits to the work they decide upon for each Sprint, they need to focus on actually doing that work. In life, people and events will constantly seek to derail our focus. Their boss might ask them to do something; that friend in sales just needs a tiny thing. And it is so easy to do. *Oh, this won't take that long. I'll just do this one thing, even though it isn't in our Sprint Backlog.*

That, my friends, is the road to not getting anything done. The goal of Scrum is twice the work in half the time. You cannot achieve that without extreme focus. In Scrum you are committed to delivering value in a very short Timebox of a week or two. You have to be focused to achieve that.

The Team needs to focus on the work they are doing and the results they want to achieve. They have to focus on continuously getting better. Everything else is just noise. We've all had those moments in our lives when we are in the zone. Work seems to flow effortlessly. We work in perfect synchrony with our Team as we create. We've all been there, and we all kinda wish it was like that all the time. But it requires focus.

It reminds me of this novelist. A pretty good one, and prolific.

Every single weekday he gets up, heads down to his office, closes the door, and starts writing by 8:00 a.m. sharp. He focuses intently on it for four hours. Then he stops. "Some days the muse shows up," he says. "Some days she doesn't. But if I wasn't sitting there and focusing on the work I was attempting, she'd never have the opportunity."

Openness

One of the pillars of Scrum is transparency. Meetings are open. Backlogs are visible, in order to understand where you are headed and when you are going to get there. Everyone knows everything that is going on. And everyone needs to be heard. Only then can you actually understand when you are going to be done.

Traditionally, people almost never know when they are going to deliver. Sure, they have dates and promises, but they're almost always wrong. They're almost always late. At Microsoft back in the 1990s they actually reached the point of just saying, *I guess it will be done whenever it is going to be done.* In many companies I visit they label all their projects with green, yellow, or red lights. For months all the projects are green—until a few weeks before they're supposed to be done and they all suddenly flip to red. And everyone acts surprised, even though it happens every time. Every single class I teach I ask people about this. Universally people laugh ruefully in recognition of a story often lived. And they really have no good answer when I ask them why they keep doing this. When I tell them that's crazy, they agree. But they keep doing it anyway, hiding the truth, because that's what they've been conditioned to do.

Openness and transparency are key to overcoming that uncertainty. By making the work visible, along with where the work is at the moment, we can start to plan based on data rather than opinion.

In today's world, much of our work is invisible. It's ideas, it's code, it's designs, it's thinking through tough problems. You need to pull the invisible into the light. What work is being done? Who is doing it?

At Riccardo's this had an immediate impact on the bottom line. If you've never worked in or managed a restaurant, you may not know this, but the absolute worst thing you have to do is scheduling. It takes hours. Who can work what shift? Phone calls to see if people are available, pulling your hair out when you can staff every position but the bar, so you have to dig up a new bartender. It's maddening. I've done it.

Riccardo's is open seven days a week for three hundred and fifty days a year. They serve lunch and dinner. As you can imagine, scheduling was always a Herculean task. So what Riccardo did was simply put a huge chart up on the wall listing every shift and what staffing was needed. He then had every Team Member take the number of Post-its that reflected the number of shifts they worked and told them to figure out the schedule. It took about an hour the first time to fill in a month's worth of shifts.

"But when we were done, we had a lot of Post-its left over," Riccardo remarks, standing in front of the board that held them all. "What we realized was that managers had been allocating shifts to Team Members that the company didn't need, and nobody knew about it." What they had been doing was giving people extra shifts to make them happy, instead of going strictly by what the company actually needed. This was actually reducing profit 10 to 20 percent, easily. Restaurants have small enough margins as it is.

When Riccardo brought this to the Teams, he wasn't angry. He didn't tell them what to do. He made it transparent and said they would have to work it out.

"Within two weeks they had managed to resolve the issue and had everything sorted. We had the right amount of people working, and that was with zero interference from me." He says the Teams realized quickly that because they were part owners, there would be more profit to share if expenses went down.

"They got that straightaway," Riccardo reflected, looking away briefly and pausing. Thoughtfully he added, "And they were able to self-regulate and self-police their shift patterns and make that work. Not just that, but they ended up with a much happier Team."

Taiichi Ohno, the creator of the Toyota Production System, famously said, "Having no problems is the worst problem of all." There are always problems. We are surrounded by problems. If you don't know what your problems are, it is impossible to fix them.

This is countercultural to many organizations. People typically are punished for the very existence of problems, regardless of their actual source. Predictably, they hide problems. They don't admit they exist. They pretend they aren't there. Worst of all, this pattern becomes so ingrained that people stop being able to perceive the problems exist at all. In Scrum, you have to be open about problems, even celebrate the revelation of problems. And sometimes they are tough! But that's great, because that's where the biggest reward lies. As Heather Timm, one of the Product Owners at Scrum Inc., tells her Team, "Sometimes you have to dive into the wreck to get to the treasure. The problem was always there; it just wasn't visible. It may be tough, but the jewels lie under the sunken ship."

It's easy to run Scrum without this kind of openness. You could have a Team in a room for a Daily Scrum, and if all they say is, *I did this yesterday, doing this today, no problems,* the whole event could be over in thirty seconds. Or less if your Team is the right size, four or five people. Don't let that happen. In a company doing Scrum right, you're going to hear lots of problems. People will be arguing sometimes. There will be a crackling energy as people wrestle with real issues.

It can be difficult for people to have the psychological safety (to use a recently popularized phrase) to talk about problems. As a leader, you have to create a culture that rewards that. Otherwise people will just keep on lying to you.

Respect

To create the environment for the transparency needed to actually get things done, people have to respect each other and, furthermore, treat each other with respect. In order to get people to be open, to admit when things aren't going well, they need to know they won't be punished for it. You must alleviate fear with respect.

You have to respect people as they are, with their strengths and weaknesses. It is so easy to judge other people. It is so easy to look at people with disdain when they admit error or lack of knowledge. It is so easy to think of yourself as better than. But there is nothing more corrosive to any relationship than a lack of respect.

There are so many companies—heck, so many relationships—that don't have respect. That are rooted in a culture of blame: *You did this. You failed at that.* Consequently, everyone is always trying to cover up, to hide from punishment, to lie.

In order to get the openness, you have to respect the person for whatever they are bringing to the table, particularly if they are bringing a problem to the table. You want to work on the problem and not blame the person.

Riccardo says he only recently faced this problem at the restaurant. They'd hired someone new who just wasn't that good. So the Team decided to give him the worst shifts. "Constructive dismissal" is what he calls it: make life so difficult for someone they'll eventually just quit.

So he asked the staff whether they had given him proper feedback. Had they talked to this person and tried to salvage him instead of treating him as if he didn't matter at all? Riccardo says that in the past he might have thrown up his hands and said he just couldn't deal with it. But "Scrum allows you to diagnose how to fix it. Now I just say, 'Fixing this problem is the number one backlog item. Fix this!'"

Riccardo says he tells Team Members they can't make a mistake. "If you make a decision and implement it, just tell us what you've done, and we'll discuss how it went. And," he notes, "so far there's not been one costly mistake. If anything, customers are much happier. They notice the Teams are much happier, even at times when we're stressed and under a lot of pressure."

Give people the freedom of knowing they aren't going to be blamed. That you have respect for them, their ideas, and their decisions.

Courage

Being open, putting your problems on the table, being transparent—that requires the ability to take risk. Change requires risk. As we see more and more companies transform from a traditional structure to an Agile structure, we see managers become afraid. Many of them don't have the courage to make that transition, because their jobs will change. The future will be different.

None of the other values matter without courage. You can't be committed, focused, open, and respectful of other people if you don't have the courage to face the downside. Change is hard. It is disruptive. It can bring long-held beliefs into a startling new—and at times not kind—light. But with the courage to change, leadership can fundamentally reshape their company to face a modern, changing, and sometimes scary world.

Here's the great thing about Scrum that some don't appreciate:

you've got a safety net. You are never investing in or committing to more than one Sprint's worth of work. You're not saying this is the way it is going to be in the future. You are not saying that is the way a billion dollars is going to be spent. You're not saying this is how this person's relationship will work forever. You're committing to trying it for a little while to see if it works. If it doesn't, you can try something else. When people realize that, it takes a huge load off their shoulders. With Scrum, you quickly see what doesn't work. Instead of wasting a billion dollars, you catch your faulty assumptions early.

Value Values

Where Scrum doesn't work well, we don't see these values in practice. And if you do want to get twice the work done in half the time, if you do want to realize the potential benefits, you have to embrace the values.

One way of making sure you are thinking about the values is to use them in your Sprint Retrospective. Write the values on the top of a whiteboard, then halfway down draw a horizontal line. Have the Team put up Post-its for the things that happened that Sprint for each value: positive goes above the line, negative below. We often recommend this approach to new Teams, and we find that patterns quickly emerge: Teams will rapidly identify the values they need to work on.

Minimum Viable Bureaucracy

After you've turned your managers into leaders, they need to create an environment that ensures the Scrum values are present. This is when you strike out at the bureaucracy that slows things down and frustrates everyone. But what structure should you have? Where do you begin?

If you are working in a traditional organization, I imagine it is something like this. There are business units, maybe regions, maybe functions, maybe lines of business. And when they want something, they ask the project management office (PMO), the one that reports to the business. That office requests stuff from an IT PMO, or an R&D PMO, or whatever. And within those PMOs they have a bunch of specialist teams that focus only on one piece of the product. There are layers upon layers of structure and lines of who reports to whom.

That's a huge amount of waste, but the part I want to focus on now is the structure itself. All the reporting, the handoffs, and the chains are just waste. They only slow things down. For the most part you do need some hierarchy, because you don't want chaos, but you want just enough hierarchy—the minimal viable bureaucracy.

To accomplish this, the leadership team first needs to set up some sort of Executive Action Team that is charged with changing the organization. I usually tell clients that this Team needs to be able to fundamentally change the company without asking for permission. You need a Team that can get things done. So you'll need legal, HR, business, technology, whomever, but the people you need to pick for this Team are the ones whose decisions will stick. And it's this Team that needs to decide where to begin.

Usually they begin with one project or product where the Teams control the whole value stream. From idea to execution, the whole thing. This might involve just a few Teams or it might be many, but you want the group to be able to independently deliver to a customer.

Let me give you an example from a partner of mine, Fabian Schwartz. He works all over Latin America. One company he was working with was the gas division of the Drummond Company in Colombia. They wanted to speed up the drilling of gas wells. The problem wasn't the drilling. No, the problems were inadequate communication and collaboration. The right information or documents weren't being passed along, or decisions weren't being made at the right moment. They were wasting huge amounts of time.

They hired Fabian to see what he could do. He decided he wouldn't even touch the actual drilling operations. The technology is pretty mature, and they weren't planning on inventing new methods. That would be really expensive. But, he thought, in any project, where is the easiest place to make change? It's at the beginning, when uncertainty is high and the cost of change is low.

So he took the senior leadership and formed them into a Scrum Team: legal, environmental, business, people in the field. The local VP was the PO. The drilling of a well had a backlog that involved exploration, acquisition, legal, development plan, permitting—all the numerous things that had to be done before a hole could be dug in the earth.

That Executive Action Team met every single day for fifteen minutes. They did all the Scrum events: they planned, they reviewed, they did the Retrospective. They set up video chats for the remote Teams in the field. And they found something quite interesting: issues that before had taken them weeks to resolve now took hours. The whole group focused on delivering a working well, rather than having each person concentrate on their piece of the puzzle. Motivation went up. Transparency increased. Simply from talking to each other and wrestling with hard problems together.

Before they did this, their average drill time took nineteen days; the fastest they had ever done it was ten days. After Scrum, the average well now takes six days. The average is now three times as fast. They didn't change any technology. They didn't change any people. They only changed how they were working.

"Scrum has been a successful implementation for our organization," said Alberto Garcia, vice president for hydrocarbons at Drummond in Colombia, "and will be implemented in other specific oil and gas operating teams: drilling, stimulation and completion, construction of production facilities."

As a leader, you have to constantly look at your organization and make incremental changes toward getting to where you want to be. It never really ends. But you need to be able to eliminate what we call organizational debt—the rules and silos and structures that are slowing you down. Leadership should be focused on that every single day.

You also have to set up a mechanism for getting the impediments that Teams identify to rise up to the Executive Action Team and be dealt with immediately. Each day Scrum Masters across your organization should be funneling up impediments that the Team can't solve. It should be fast. Just as the individual Teams have a daily meeting for fifteen minutes, they send a representative to a Scaled Daily Scrum for fifteen minutes. If you do it right, you can coordinate a couple thousand people in about an hour.

Let me give you a quick example. I mentioned back in Chapter 1 how Saab Aerospace is building a fighter plane from the ground up, the Gripen E. This is how they do Scaled Daily Scrum. At 7:30 in the morning, every day, each Team has their Daily Scrum. At 7:45 the Scrum Masters from those Teams go to that Scaled Daily Scrum with the impediments and dependencies that can't be resolved at the Team level. At 8:00 a representative from each of those goes to another scaled level with the issues that they can't handle. At 8:15 there is another. At 8:30 the Executive Action Team, the leadership of the whole project, gets the problems that only they can fix. Their remit is to fix them within twenty-four hours. They coordinate about two thousand people in less than an hour. And the leadership views it as critical cost control. They see their job as getting that plane out the door as fast as possible, and anything that slows the Teams down, keeping them out of flow, is cost.

But maybe you don't need five layers. Maybe you need two for some areas, maybe just one for something else. You only want to coordinate what you absolutely have to. Hierarchy and structure, but only just enough. As leadership, you want fast feedback loops from the bottom of the organization. That will give you the ability to shift and change things fast. Speed is a force multiplier.

Innovating the How

Speed matters. Everywhere. Picture this. You have a hospital. A good one. No, an excellent one. Your care and outcomes are second to none. You've got Nobel winners on staff.

You have a few dozen operating rooms at this hospital. Rooms where lives are saved and wounds healed. How many operations you can do in each room determines how many people you can help.

Listen, I know it isn't sexy. But a key question for a hospital is how long it takes to clean and reset an operating room. Which means really clean. The lights, the floor, the walls, the entire environment. People's lives depend on just how clean the room is.

It takes about an hour. And it has for decades. From "wheels out" to "wheels in," from a patient being rolled out of the room to when a new patient can be rolled in. About an hour.

So you—well, they, this hospital—called us to see if we could partner with Alexa, their process improvement guru, and help.

Scrum Inc.'s Kevin Ball is an ex-Marine, a jazz aficionado, and someone who rips apart process to produce results. He looked at that hour as a challenge.

Now, this is no easy task. Think about it. It's not just sterilizing the room. They need to coordinate with the next medical team, the surgeon, anesthesiologist, and nurses, in order to have the right surgical instruments set up in the right place.

Kevin spent the first day observing the process. "We were just working with the cleaning crew at first," Kevin recalls. Then on day two, he asked the crew members this question, "What do you think you can do to improve the process?"

They were reluctant to answer at first. But then ideas began to surface. The members of the cleaning crew had each been doing just one task. They soon realized that if they partnered on the same task it would get done faster. Repeat that cooperation and the total time it took to clean the room would decrease significantly. For two days they tried this experiment, and it worked again and again.

Kevin then expanded their work to include the others involved in turning around each operating room. More efficiencies were found, from the handoff between surgical teams to just when the nurse pushes a button to signify that it is time to bring the next patient in.

The results were clear. The "wheels out" to "wheels in" time had been cut in half. From an average of about an hour to half an hour, sometimes less. All without sacrificing quality.

I could give you the numbers on how much money the hospital saved, or how much more they made. But to me, those aren't terribly important. Kevin made it possible for this hospital to save more lives and treat more people. Not by changing technology. Or adding staff. Solely by looking at the small things. The process.

And refusing to believe it couldn't be made better.

Oh, and it took two weeks.

With Great Power Comes Great Responsibility

As leadership, you not only have to support your Teams, remove their impediments, and keep them happy. You also have to hold them accountable. On the standard annual performance review, with its fifty dimensions rated on a scale of 1 to 5, only 10 percent of your people can be top performers, because obviously people fall neatly into a bell curve. You know the one. Pretty much the only thing that does is demotivate people. How do we do it in Scrum? Scrum Inc.'s Kim Antelo put a performance review together for a large oil services company, and we've been using it ever since. You only have to ask a few questions, and the data is pretty easy to find.

SCRUM MASTERS

- Are they actually doing Scrum—three roles, five events, three artifacts, five values?

- Is there a Team working agreement? Has the Team documented their Team norms and behaviors?

- Is Velocity being measured? Is it increasing by at least 10 percent quarter over quarter?

- Is Team Happiness being measured as a leading indicator?

- Are they improving Scrum at the company beyond just their Team?

- Are they continuously learning?

PRODUCT OWNERS

- Is more value being delivered by the Team's speed? In other words, is more money being made from the same amount of work because the right things are being made and delivered to customers at the right time?

- Are they meeting key success criteria for their product or service?

- Do they quickly kill products that don't meet success criteria fast enough? (This last bit is incredibly important. So many projects lumber on like zombies, feasting on people and money for years because no one wants to admit they were a bad idea.)

TEAM MEMBERS

- Are they building the thing right? Is quality increasing?
- Are they becoming skilled at more than one thing, branching out from their limited specialty?
- Are they teaching other Team Members their expertise?

LEADERS

- Are they providing clear vision?
- Are they growing people and careers?
- Are the people who report to them happy and excited about coming to work?
- Are their Teams organized in the best way possible to deliver value?
- Do their Teams have all the skills and tools they need?
- Are they holding their Product Owners and Scrum Masters accountable?

Scrum gives people great freedom of action. They decide how they will work and how much they will work. They are expected to manage and organize themselves. That's great. But the key thing is delivery. Are they having an impact?

You want multiple paths to leadership. Not the number of people you manage, but the impact of outcomes you are influencing. You want people to be able to grow in your organization and to be respected as an individual contributor if they can influence outcomes that affect the business. You need to have clear paths to success that focus on outcomes, customer success, great products, and fantastic ideas, not on clawing one's way to middle management.

Speaking of them, let's talk about them.

The Insurgent Resistance

Scrum is pretty easy to convince teams to do. It makes their lives better. They get to have more fun. A lot of the nonsense is taken out of the way. They get to make great stuff. They get to do the great things that ignited their career in the first place.

Senior leadership is also usually pretty easy to convince. *Twice the work in half the time? I'm in. Happier people, faster to market, protect myself from being disrupted? Sign me up.*

Middle management, though . . . they can be tough. They are the persistent challenge in any company that is trying to transform. There are a few reasons for this, but you have to be very aware of these reasons and deal with them quickly, or middle managers will completely derail any efforts at change.

For one thing, they can feel threatened: *This Scrum thing may expose some problems that have been around for a long time. I might have caused those problems. I'm not too sure about that whole transparency thing.*

Or it might be: *The way things are now, I have a pretty good line of sight to my bonus and my promotion. What if I'm not good at this? Will my job be at risk?* In a way they're right. Their roles are certainly at risk. You simply will need fewer middle managers. That doesn't mean you fire them all, but you do need to think about how they can serve by delivering value instead of managing people.

And they will kill you with passive-aggressive noncompliance. In public they'll be behind the changes, but behind the scenes they will be spreading poison. This can happen even at high levels in an organization. People can't lead if they don't believe in the change. And if they don't believe in it, they will wait: *Oh, in a little while they won't be looking at me. This too shall pass. I'll keep my head down and only pretend to change. I will survive.*

Don't tolerate that for a second. You really do have to have people who are passionate about making a serious change in how they work. When clients ask me about people who are simply resistant and don't want to change, I tell them that there are rules about coming to work. Some of them aren't optional. And is one person's discomfort worth putting your entire company at risk? Because that is the choice you are making.

Change Your Culture, Change Your Limits

An amazing thing, to me anyway, is that once you reshape your structure, a new culture emerges. Organizations, families, people—we are all complex adaptive systems. Understanding each individual component does not give you an understanding of the whole. The culture emerges from the interactions of the various pieces, and that can be quite startling—the end state may be something far greater than you can currently imagine.

As you free yourself from the rigid structural operating models that have been artificially imposed for one reason or another, it changes what you are capable of doing. Not only will you finally be able to get done the stuff you want done, but you'll be able to do things you couldn't have imagined before.

Remember, the structure will emerge. Don't think you can get the impact Scrum can truly deliver just by changing a bunch of job titles. That's making the fundamental mistake of thinking you know the answer ahead of time. You don't. The right organizational architecture will emerge as you endeavor to deliver more value faster to customers. That's what really matters. Like with

Adobe, the Rijksmuseum, Apple, Google, or Amazon, you need to get close enough to the customer to see how you should organize yourself to deliver the best experience, service, or product that you can.

Riccardo is now beginning two new projects—restaurants run solely by Scrum. "Everything will be Scrum. The design process. Recruitment. Everything," he says. He excitedly talks about Stable Teams for both the front of the house and the kitchen. Weekly Sprints. The chef will be the Product Owner. The Scrum Master will be the first person in the door, checking for impediments: Do the phones and computers work? Did the deliveries arrive? What could possibly slow the Team down today?

Without Scrum, Riccardo says, he would have left the business. Now he can see how to scale. Two restaurants. Three. More. The world is open again.

As an organization becomes Agile, short feedback loops inform decisions, and the whole place becomes alive. We are capable of so much, yet we hold ourselves back. I understand why. I do it myself. We become so used to our current way of thinking, our current way of doing, our way of communicating with each other, that we are as blind to it as we are to the air we breathe. But by taking concrete, incremental steps, bit by bit, week by week, we can transform ourselves and our organizations into something remarkable.

THE TAKEAWAY

Structure is culture. And your culture defines your limits. A rigid structure begets a rigid cultural and product architecture. It makes change dramatically more difficult. That's true at the team level, but it is even more true and more important at the organizational level.

Management must become leadership. Leaders need to have a compelling vision, a compelling direction, a way forward into the undiscovered country, and they need to communicate that out to their people. They need their people to be excited about what they are doing. This could be changing the world, delivering a better product in a new way that will disrupt the market, or simply getting their great ideas out the door faster than they ever could before.

Value openness and transparency. In today's world, much of our work is invisible. It's ideas, it's code, it's designs, it's thinking through tough problems. You need to pull the invisible into the light. What work is being done? Who is doing it? Openness and transparency are key to overcoming uncertainty. By making the work visible, along with the state of the work at any given moment, we can start to plan based on data rather than opinion.

Be courageous. You can't be committed, focused, open, and respectful of other people if you don't have the courage to face the downside. Change is hard. But with the courage to change, leadership can fundamentally reshape their company to face a modern, changing, and sometimes scary world.

BACKLOG

- How would you describe the structure of your organization? Identify how it is having a positive or negative effect on the products you make or the services you deliver. How would you change that organizational structure for the better?

- Are you a manager or a leader? Think hard about this one. Do you dictate or empower? Do you force compliance or share your vision? Do you make decisions or improve them?

- List three items of organizational debt at your workplace. Now figure out how to remove them.

- Use the Scrum values in your daily work. Encourage others to do so. What effect do they have?

CHAPTER 7

Doing It Right

Sometimes the hardest part of fixing a problem is wrestling with the words to use to describe the problem, let alone proffer a solution. Christopher Alexander is a hugely influential architect who fought his way through the same issue when trying to talk about why something works in a building or a place. Sometimes places just feel *right*. It could be a room. It could be a street corner. It could be a place to work. He wanted a language to describe the things you could do in design to create what he called the "quality without a name." When a place is just the Platonic ideal of that particular type of place.

His theories about design reshaped how communities, buildings, and systems are built. In the early 1970s, Alexander tried to define common solutions to common problems that will work every time in multiple contexts. He wanted people to be able to talk about them clearly and succinctly. In 1977 he published *A Pattern Language: Towns, Buildings, Construction*, which listed hundreds of these patterns, enough to make a language itself.

Each pattern describes a problem that occurs over and over again in our environment, and then describes the core of the solution to that problem, in such a way that you can use this solution a million times over, without ever doing it the same way twice.

Let me give you an example from Alexander's book:

Pattern 150: A Place to Wait
The process of waiting has inherent conflict in it.

He then laments the current state of waiting. It doesn't really matter what we're waiting for—a bus, a doctor's appointment, a train. We spend a lot of time waiting, and it sucks. And we can't fully check out, because we don't know for sure when what we are waiting for will happen. So we can't leave and come back later. We're stuck there. And the typical waiting room is usually kind of dreary. But, asks Alexander, what if we could change that and make waiting a positive experience, a rewarding period of free time? What if "with the support of the surroundings [a person] is able to draw into himself, become still, meditative"?

Therefore, the pattern is:

In places where people end up waiting (for a bus, for an appointment, for a plane), create a situation which makes the waiting positive. Fuse the waiting with some other activity—newspaper, coffee, pool tables, horseshoes; something which draws people in who are not simply waiting. And also the opposite: make a place which can draw a person waiting into a reverie; quiet; a positive silence.

The pattern A Place to Wait links to other patterns, like Street Windows, Street Cafe, and Office Connections. Every pattern links to another pattern, creating a syntax of solutions. As my father, Jeff Sutherland, put it:

> A Pattern Language is an attempt to express deeper wisdom through a set of interconnected expressions arising from contextual knowledge. It moves beyond a list of processes, to seek activities or qualities that repeat across many of those processes, in an effort to find what works. It is an interconnected whole that, when applied coherently, creates "the quality that has no name." Combining multiple patterns creates a whole greater than the sum of the individual patterns.[1]

Teams That Finish Early Accelerate Faster

A few years back a few guys over at OpenView Venture Partners came to Scrum Inc. with a conundrum. They had thought Scrum was about Velocity: How fast is the Team going? Can they get more done in each and every Sprint? So they loaded up their Teams with enough backlog that they could finish it in a Sprint, although it would certainly take until the last day. Then they noticed something. The Teams that did that kept the same Velocity, they got the same amount of work done, but they didn't get the fourfold improvement in productivity that was the design goal of Scrum. Other Teams, the Teams that finished their Sprints early, they got faster and faster. Eventually they realized that Scrum isn't about Velocity; it's about Acceleration.

That was the pattern:

Teams that finish early accelerate faster.

Teams often take too much work into a Sprint and cannot finish it.

Failure to attain the Sprint Goal prevents the team from improving.[2]

Working with a group of experts at the Scrum Pattern Language Project, we came up with a pattern language for hyperproductive Teams. These patterns are ones that have been used in multiple companies, multiple domains, multiple times. These practices are the core of executing Scrum well.

You Can Have Data Without Information, but You Can't Have Information Without Data

That saying, quoted over and over by data scientists like a mantra, was coined by the computer scientist, novelist, and big data guru Daniel Keys Moran. And it is the problem that 3M Health Information Systems is trying to address for hospitals, insurance companies, and health plans. Just to give you one example: Under the Affordable Care Act, hospitals can be penalized by the federal government if they have high rates of readmission or hospital-acquired infections, among other issues. It's part of a movement away from volume-based care, where a hospital is paid by the number of procedures and tests (a fee-for-service model), and toward value-based care, which pays based on patient results (measuring outcomes rather than outputs). In 2017, 751 hospitals got their Medicare reimbursement money cut because they didn't meet the new standards.

One of the standards is preventable readmissions. That's when a person goes to the hospital for something and then is readmitted to the hospital a few days or weeks later for something that could have been prevented by better-quality care, better discharge planning, better follow-up after leaving the hospital, or better communication between the inpatient and outpatient healthcare teams.

If only there was some way to know which patients were likely to be readmitted, as a very small percentage of patients drive the vast majority of readmissions. The key question, of course, is how do you know if a patient is likely to fall into that group? Enter 3M Health Information Systems (3M HIS). They are a massive big-data operation. They look at all the data, from doctors' notes to lab reports to demographic data—all sorts of stuff—and help hospitals take proactive rather than reactive measures to give patients the support they need. People are healthier, not as many people are cycling in and out of the ER, costs are lower, and there are better outcomes for everyone. Cool, no?

In September 2014 my father and I published our first book, *Scrum: The Art of Doing Twice the Work in Half the Time*. It landed on many people's desks that fall. Two of them were David Frazee and Tammy Sparrow at 3M HIS. David was the chief technology officer of the division, Tammy his number two. They gave the book to everyone on the executive team. And then they gave us a call.

In May 2015 they brought us in to assess the state of their Scrum, which wasn't good. They also had a crisis looming: in October of that year one of their core products would have to radically change, and their confidence they would meet that deadline was not high.

Struck by Duck, Subsequent Encounter

W61.62XD is the code that indicates an unfortunate incident with a duck and the subsequent encounter with a physician, which we don't like to talk about. That code is really important. It is part of the ICD-10, the International Classification of Disease version 10. Fine, technically the International Statistical Classification of Diseases and Related Health Problems. Let's stick with ICD. There are thousands of these codes, around 141,000. The World Health Organization uses these codes to classify just about anything that can go wrong with the human body, such as V97.33XD: Sucked into jet engine, subsequent encounter. Or Y93.D: Activities involving arts and handicrafts. Or the tragically common V91.07XD: Burn due to water-skis on fire, subsequent encounter.

In 2015, the U.S. system was finally going to change from ICD-9 to ICD-10. ICD-9 had about 14,000 codes, an order of magnitude less than ICD-10. These codes are really important to the healthcare system, because this data can provide huge insights into what is actually happening to people out there. It's also how insurance companies determine what they are going to pay for and how much they'll pay for it. Perhaps they won't cover Y92.146: Swimming pool of prison as the place of occurrence of the external cause. That's right—a specific code for injuries suffered in a swimming pool in a prison. Thankfully there are also codes for a prison dining room, bathroom, and kitchen as the place of occurrence.

At the time, 3M HIS had some five thousand customers using their system to accurately determine all these codes so that hospitals and clinics could get reimbursement from the insurance company or the government. The deadline for the ICD-10 switch was October 1, 2015. And it wasn't looking good.

We started working with the leadership of the division that summer. That's when Tammy got her new job title: Director, Agile Journey. Now she oversees quality and commercialization as well. The first thing we told 3M HIS was that they didn't know how to prioritize. They had people working on too many things at once, even though it was clear that ICD-10 was their top priority. Working with Tammy and David, we launched five Teams to meet that deadline. It was tense: this deadline was not optional, and either their flagship product would work or it would not.

W55.29XA: Other contact with cow, subsequent encounter. There are other codes for "bitten by cow" and "kicked by cow." We don't talk about this incident either. Like the duck.

October 1 came and the lights didn't go out. Over the next

year, using the Teams That Finish Early Accelerate Faster pattern, they increased their Velocity 160 percent. Now they have hundreds of people on Scrum Teams. What the pattern does, says Tammy, is force your Teams to track what they do, get things out of their way, and let them focus. "You can finish faster with that focus. The goal is not to overburden Teams, but to get Teams able to get the work done."

So let's go through the patterns that will accelerate your Teams too.

Stable Teams

Stakeholders are happiest with teams who can meet their expectations in a timely fashion, so the team wants to do what is necessary to reduce variance in its predictions.

Therefore: Keep teams stable and avoid shuffling people around between teams. Stable Teams tend to get to know their capacity, which makes it possible for the business to have some predictability. Dedicate team members to a single team whenever possible.[3]

Here's how it happens. Usually. Maybe it will sound familiar anyway. You've been working on this project with a great team. You jell, you get along, you crush the work. That team is a finely tuned engine built for speed. We've all been on a team like this at least once in our lives. It's an amazing experience. Unforgettable.

The one that comes to mind for me was a group of people who launched and produced a live radio talk show at WBUR in Boston called *The Connection*. We all sat in an office that was surely a fire code violation. We were on the phones, banging out scripts, coming up with creative new ideas, putting out two shows a day, every day, without a break or a repeat of topic. Man, that was fun. We were the talk of the town. You could walk into any bar in the city and people would be discussing what had been on *The Connection* that day. It was heady. We fought not infrequently. We laughed more. I worked secret messages into the scripts that only my girlfriend (now wife) would get. We would have a guest back out fifteen minutes to air, and we would instantly leap into action, hammering out another idea in mere minutes. We knew each other's talents and minds so well that we always knew someone would catch the ball we threw without looking. I'll never forget it.

But what happens? In most companies, when the project ends, that great team you were just remembering? They break them up and put new teams together for the next project. But you know what? It takes a long time to become a highly functional team.

Bruce Tuckman was a professor of educational psychology at Ohio State University. One of his more influential pieces of work was a 1965 paper titled "Developmental Sequence in Small Groups." In it he reviewed dozens of studies of group formation, and he found that teams go through four stages as they become a team. The first he called "forming." He described it as a time when the team members test each other. They test the boundaries of interpersonal dynamics and how other members of the team approach their work.

Tuckman describes the second stage, "storming," this way:

> The second point in the sequence is characterized by conflict and polarization around interpersonal issues, with concomitant emotional responding in the task sphere. These behaviors serve as resistance to group influence and task requirements and may be labeled as storming.[4]

I love that phrasing: "concomitant emotional responding in the task sphere." Basically, people get angry with each other. They feel the need to create edges and borders between themselves and others. And it usually comes out as either quiet seething or finally just losing your temper. You've done it. It's okay, everyone has.

The third stage, "norming," is when those arguments are resolved. Boundaries are established, and groups start building cohesion. People begin identifying themselves with their team. New roles might be adopted as the team figures out how best to work together. It's setting up the way the team has agreed to work.

Tuckman describes "performing," the fourth stage, as when the structure of the team becomes the tool of how the team gets stuff done. I love that. The sociodynamics of the group become the energy the team uses to produce great work. Who actually does what becomes less important than that the team as a whole does it.

That doesn't happen quickly. It takes a long time to go through the process of building trust, and knowledge of each other's knowledge, and a positive culture, and acceptable behaviors and ways of working together. It just takes time. There are a bunch of reasons for this, and boy, has this been studied.

The first is the idea of a shared mental model. I'll spare you the dry scientific language, but basically the idea is that when a group learns enough about their team, they can anticipate what other team members are going to need or what they are going to do. They've gained an implicit understanding of the group dynamic.

Another theory posited about why teams that work together for a long time are successful is the concept of transactive memory, first studied in couples who are romantically involved (a "dyadic" relationship, is the term used in the literature, and now the name of my next band): how shared experiences create memories that require both partners in order to be fully recollected. The classic example is one partner asking another, "Where was that place where we had that duck?" (W61.62XD: Struck by duck, subsequent encounter. Remember, we don't like to talk about it.) And the partner responds,

"Oh, you mean when Jim and Sally were there and you got a little too tipsy?" "That was it!" "Oh, that was in Brooklyn."

As a group, the team stores pieces of memory in different people. The team members come to rely upon each other for that. They likely don't even realize they are doing it. But shared experiences build shared memory, which creates a new thing that exists only in the relationship between people, what Professor Ikujiro Nonaka calls *ba*. Interestingly, the science says that this can't happen if the group is too big, because the shared memory network has a size limit. It's about seven people. Hmmmmm. Same size as a Scrum Team. Isn't that interesting.

One meta-analysis of the literature on this looked at all the research and wrote in conclusion:

> Beyond familiarity, shared experience, and face-to-face interaction, the research base to help identify techniques for enhancing transactive memory is as yet not sufficiently developed to warrant specific recommendations for how to enhance it in teams.

Familiarity, shared experience, and face-to-face interaction: this is what Scrum is trying to put a framework around. To create on purpose, rather than have it happen by happy accident. Stable, co-located, cross-functional teams: that's the secret. It's not complicated.

I could go on about forming team cohesion, team pride, leadership effects, training. There are all sorts of things they've studied in the effort to help build a great team. The first thing, though, is Stable Teams.

Another important part of Team stability is team dedication. You don't want people on two Teams or three or five. Fractional assignment will halve the productivity of your Teams.

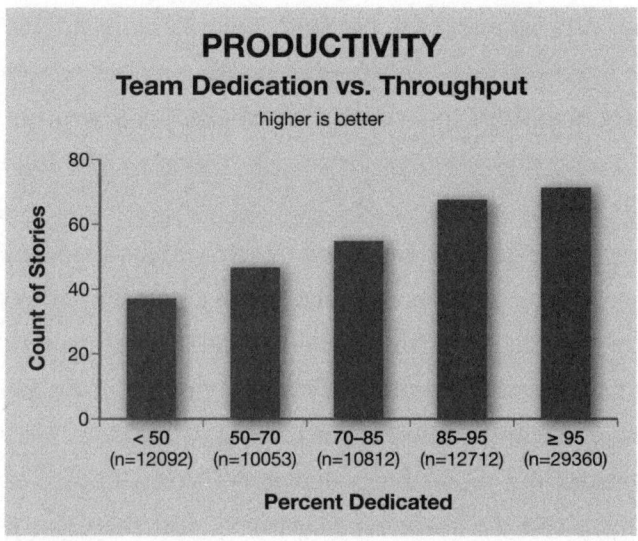

Rally Software Development Corp. "The Impact of Agile Quantified," 2015 (online).

That's data from more than 75,000 Teams. This comes from Rally, one of the big online Scrum tools. They looked into their data—they have a lot of it—and found that if a Team has members that are fully dedicated to that Team, they are nearly twice as productive as Teams made up of people who are working on more than one Team at a time.

This is obvious, but everyone does it: *Oh, Lucinda is the only person who knows this, so she'll work on five Teams.* It kills poor Lucinda, who has to drastically context-shift every day. Not just different work, but different people. Frankly, it's not only inefficient, it's cruel. It prevents Lucinda from having the benefits of a Team, enjoying *ba* and shared memory.

At 3M HIS before Scrum, they had Stable Teams, but the Team members weren't dedicated to a single team. "Most people had to work on half a dozen Teams or projects," says David, now the director of corporate research systems at 3M. "We immediately pushed to get at least 80 percent of the people dedicated to a single project. There was an immediate effect of clarity and what was expected," he told me. "The ICD-10 project was, one could argue, the 'never-waste-a-crisis' opportunity. We turned it around in a matter of weeks." A few months later they had more than twenty Teams. Nothing speaks louder than success.

Tammy does point out that sometimes people take Stable Teams a bit too seriously. She says they should be about 80 percent stable; keep them together too long and they start to stagnate. Usually some shift happens naturally in Teams as people move jobs or get promoted or whatnot, but it is something to look out for.

The great thing about this is that establishing Stable Teams is an easy fix. You can do it almost overnight, and the effects are immediate and dramatic.

Yesterday's Weather

It's human nature that individuals and teams with self-esteem set increasingly higher goals for themselves. And it's also human nature for teams to overreach their abilities, and they end either taking shortcuts to avoid disappointing themselves and their stakeholders, or fail to deliver what they expected.

Therefore: In most cases, the number of Estimation Points completed in the last Sprint is a reliable predictor of how many Estimation Points of work the team will complete in the next Sprint.[5]

Basically, the best predictor of future performance is past performance. Estimation points are just a way of sizing how much effort a piece of work will take. Big things take a lot of points, little things a small number. Basically, if your Team got ten backlog items done last Sprint, bring only ten in for the next Sprint. It's simple, but Teams hate it. People want to improve. They want to prove they can do better.

Sure, sometimes they can. But you know what, sometimes they can't. And it is far better to finish early, pull more work in, and have the possibility to *accelerate*. Not finishing what you set out to do is a morale crusher. You beat yourself up about it, even if you knew it was a stretch.

Often management insists on stretch goals, to push the Team or the organization. The problem is that if you say the goal is X, people will do whatever it takes to achieve X. It can lead to taking shortcuts, or even knowingly doing the wrong thing so that it *seems* you achieved X. Remember the whole lying bit?

We recommend taking the average Velocity of the last three Sprints, not simply of the last one. It's a noisy metric subject to a lot of variables, so averaging it quiets the noise.

And remember, you can't finish early if you commit to everything. Part of Scrum is saying no.

It wasn't that teams pulled too much work at 3M HIS; it was management. "Before Scrum," says David, "people were overcommitted. It was a classic case where the business wants to deliver this by a certain date, and the technical teams simply could not do all the requested work in that time." Once they had actual Velocity data, they were able to push back against that, saying, *This is what we are capable of.* It also gave leadership a much better idea of when something would actually be done.

"One problem I do see," Tammy notes, "is that Teams will sometimes change their estimates to fit more work into a Sprint, but they sacrifice quality." She wants Teams to push back, to insist on Yesterday's Weather so they can build quality in rather than try to fix it later.

Swarming

Working on too many things at once can radically reduce individual effectiveness, team Velocity, or enterprise well-being. It can cripple Velocity and can sometimes reduce it to zero.

Therefore: Focus maximum team effort on one item in the Product Backlog and get it done as soon as possible.[6]

Earlier, I talked about the difference between being busy and being done. This pattern is the one that fixes that.

Here's the simple truth: humans love distractions. We're like dogs with squirrels or magpies with shiny objects: every time we see one, we leap on it. We all know this. I certainly hope that by now people have internalized not only the notion that multitasking is bad but also the idea that trying to do more than one thing at a time kills productivity. Every time we get interrupted by an email or switch from one task to another (*Hey, did someone just say something wrong on the Internet that I must correct right now?*), our focus collapses. It can take hours to get back into the frame of mind of what we were doing. This is true at the individual level, but it is also true at the Team level and at the organizational level. Let's start with the Team.

Let me take you back to the founder of the Toyota Production System, Taiichi Ohno. He had a taxonomy of waste, things that slowed the system. He divided them up into *muda*, *mura*, and *muri*. *Muda* translates from the Japanese as "no result"—unfinished work. *Mura* translates as "inconsistency or unevenness"—it is actually a term from textile work, referring to a snag in the cloth. And *muri* translates as "no reason." These three types of waste describe what gets in the way of getting stuff done, such as overproduction, waiting, transportation, absurd expectations, and the like.

The worst form of waste for Ohno, and truly the worst in any context, was in-process inventory. People often call it work in progress (or process, whatever), or WIP. It's the worst form of waste because you have spent time, money, and effort and you still have nothing to show for it. The work is not done.

The key is to move to what Ohno called "one-piece continuous flow," which I call "getting stuff done, fast." On any Scrum Team they'll have maybe ten or twenty things in their Sprint Backlog—the work they've committed to that Sprint. And in almost every company I've visited, all those backlog items have been started but nothing is done.

The Swarming pattern addresses this. It says to focus solely on the most important thing in the backlog and work on nothing else until it is complete. The whole Team should put their entire effort into completing one thing all the way through before they even think about doing anything else. Because they are focused on the goal, they can deliver value quickly.

Think of a Formula One pit crew. If you haven't ever seen one in action, Google a video. It's impressive. The race car pulls into the pit and comes to a complete stop. Because when the race car stops it immediately starts falling behind, the team needs to get the car in and out of the pit and back onto the raceway as fast as possible. So as soon as the car screeches to a halt, as many as twenty people go to work. Each tire requires the close synchronization of three people: one to operate the pneumatic gun to rip off the nuts holding the tires, one to take the tire off, and one to put the new tire on. Each tenth of a second counts. And that's just the wheels; the other people are making adjustments, fueling the car, anything else they can fix to get that car back on the road in seconds.

That's Swarming—total concentration by a team on delivering the value of getting a car back on the track. And that is what you want your Scrum Teams to do.

Tammy admits that 3M HIS still has problems getting all their Teams to be cross-functional and able to Swarm. Their Teams working on cloud services can do it, because it was designed modularly from the beginning. For their legacy systems, it is incredibly difficult to split up the work.

"Conway's law, for sure," she says—the product reflects the organizational architecture. But they are making changes. 3M HIS is dramatically less siloed these days—all the Teams report up into the R&D structure instead of being scattered across the business. They are investing heavily in moving to the cloud and creating a services model. But it takes time. It doesn't happen overnight.

"When I reflect on our transformation," Tammy muses, "I think about how you kept saying it is a journey. The first year or two everyone was really excited. Then it got hard." They were excited because in the beginning you get to fix the easy stuff. Later on you run into the hard problems: how the organization is structured, the architecture of the product. They're moving forward, she told me, and have big plans for how to keep transforming. But it isn't always easy.

Interrupt Buffer

Changing priorities or problems in the field often interrupts the work of Scrum teams during a Sprint. Sales and marketing demands, combined with management interference, can cause chronic dysfunction in a team, repeated failure of Sprints, failure to meet release dates, and even company failure.

Therefore: Explicitly allot time for interrupts and do not allow more work than fits within the allotment. If work exceeds the allotment, abort the Sprint.[7]

Alex Sheive is one of our coaches here at Scrum Inc. He first encountered Scrum about ten years ago, and once he saw the Interrupt pattern, he says, he knew he had to work that way. He was hired at a financial services company in July 2007—not the best time for that career move, you may recall, as Wall Street soon entered its biggest meltdown since the Great Depression. He joined a team writing tools for traders and shared an office with the lead developer of that team. His officemate was a good guy—they got along, they both worked hard. *What* they worked on changed. Frequently. One day one of the firm's seven partners would say, *This is the most important thing.* The next week, or even sometimes the next *day*, a different partner might want something totally different. Not a lot of focus. But Alex didn't think much of it. Their Team got the requests done and heard nothing but positive feedback.

Then came time for annual reviews. His officemate returned from a review meeting, slammed the door, and banged his head on their shared desk. The Team had been assigned a huge, important project at the beginning of the year and hadn't made one iota of progress on it. Because he was the lead developer, he'd been dressed down by his boss and told they had effectively accomplished nothing that year. The really weird bit, Alex says, is even though they had been working in the same room every day for six months, on the same Team, talking about work all the time, complaining about work, Alex had never once heard of this project. They had been working hard, doing what they were asked to do. It wasn't that the partners wanted to derail the project; they just didn't realize that by interrupting them for one urgent request after another, they had made it impossible for the Team to focus on the project, much less complete it. But did they take responsibility for their actions? No. To them it was obvious that the lead developer had failed.

I see this happen all too often. Teams are interrupted all the time by management, or sales, or support, and told to drop what they're working on and do this really important thing that just popped up. Then, of course, when they get to Sprint Review, nothing is done. And management thinks, *Well, that Team isn't performing.*

The solution—and this is the solution to a lot of things in Scrum—is to make the costs of decisions visible. Sometimes there are real emergencies that do need to be dealt with right away. But not everything is an emergency. So what the Team does is set aside some percentage of their capacity and call that their Interrupt Buffer. Let's say they normally get twenty backlog items done in a Sprint. Well, they should only take on fifteen for the next Sprint, leaving the rest of the space as the "In Emergency, Break Glass" reserve.

The Product Owner stands in front of that buffer as all the requests come in. Only the PO gets to decide if it is really worth it to interrupt the Team, because that will slow them down. So they might say, *That is important, but it isn't more important than the stuff in this Sprint's backlog, so we'll do it next Sprint. Or the Sprint after.* There's some stuff that really isn't important at all, and because the Product Owner owns that backlog, they can simply say, *Sure, I'll put it in the backlog! At the bottom.* But there are some things that are worth interrupting the Team for, so the PO will use up a bit of that Interrupt Buffer.

Here's the trick: when that buffer overflows, you have to abort the Sprint. Stop work immediately and re-plan what you can actually get done in the time remaining in the Sprint and what the priorities are. Because if that buffer overflows, some of the work the Team committed to in Sprint Planning *is not going to get done.* There is nothing more demoralizing to a Team than knowing they are going to fail. They know. It's pretty clear. And the worst thing is doing nothing about it.

A second-order effect of aborting the Sprint is that leadership hates it. In the sales meeting on Monday Sally might turn to Ray and say, "Why did you blow up the Sprint, Ray? Now the stuff I've promised my customers didn't get done. And it's *your* fault." Place the fault where it belongs, on the people interrupting the Team, not on the Team itself. Make it a big deal. The company will self-organize to not let that happen.

Another second-order effect is that when someone's manager does ask for something, the person can say, *Hey, it's not up to me. I'd love to help you out, but we've got these new rules—ya gotta talk to the Product Owner. If it was up to me, sure, I'd say yes, but I don't write the rules.*

Let's say the Team is trained using Scrum and is forced to abort their very first Sprint due to a large Interrupt from one of the seven partners. This time the effect of the Interrupt is *visible*. The cost of the actions of one partner can be seen by the other six. And as a result, it never happens again. The Team is able to focus on that big project they are working on and deliver it well before the end of the year. They then move on to the next most important project.

What's important is that you make the cost of decisions visible. Teams usually are held back by forces external to the Team process. Remember, the true goal is speed. Measure it and find out what is keeping you and the Team from getting faster.

The Interrupt Buffer was key in enabling 3M HIS to move from a traditional organization to an Agile one. In the beginning, maybe 60 percent of a Team's effort at 3M HIS was taken up with Interrupts. But over the years they've focused on driving it down. It's now about 20 percent. And they're thinking hard about that. They're working on those difficult changes that can get them to the next level.

Good Housekeeping

Where there's a mess, you lose time and energy determining where and what to start on.

Therefore: Maintain a completely clean product and work environment, continuously or at the end of each day.[8]

Back in 2006–2007 there were a hundred attacks on coalition forces in Iraq, mainly American, every single day. And the favorite targets of the insurgents were American convoys—there were lots of blown-up Humvees and trucks and other equipment.

One day my editor at NPR asked me, "What happens to all the stuff?"

"What do you mean?"

"Where do all those blown-up Humvees go? I mean, they're spending billions of dollars on repairs. Where are the repairs taking place?"

"I don't know. Let me find out."

It turns out that a lot of the damaged trucks end up at the Red River Army Depot, about twenty miles outside of Texarkana, Texas. Now, this will come as no surprise to those of you who have been to East Texas, but there is a whole lot of *nothing* in East Texas. As the war heated up, the Pentagon decided to shut the facility down to save money—outsource the whole thing and call it a day. Why? Because Red River could fix only three Humvees a week. And when you've got a hundred blown-up vehicles a day, three a week is not going to cut it.

Of the few thousand people who worked at the depot, only one was in uniform: the colonel in charge. The rest of the people there were civilians. These were good jobs, and the closing of the depot would be a tremendous economic blow to the area. So the colonel decided to see how companies like Ford and GM manufactured their cars. If you've never seen a Lean production line, find a video on YouTube; it's almost magical, a carefully orchestrated ballet of parts and people. It's all based on the Toyota Production System I mentioned earlier.

At Toyota, whenever there is a problem, workers are encouraged to stop the line by pulling what's called the andon cord. When that happens, management comes over—not to see how the worker messed up, but to try to discover the root cause of the problem and fix it so it *never happens again*. And slowly, bit by bit, the line becomes faster and faster and quality gets better and better. The rule is to never let a known defect go from one station to another on the line.

Let's head back to Red River. Picture this: There are blown-up Humvees everywhere—in parking lots, alongside roads, in the fields, under trees. Everywhere you look. There are also these massive World War II–era buildings that hulk all over the place. And when you go inside these buildings, you see a ballet of engines, armor, tires—they all seem to float through the air and end up at the exact right place at exactly the right time. Above each stop in the line is a big digital countdown clock set at sixteen minutes. Every sixteen minutes the Humvees have to move. Speed, with quality, is key.

The old way of fixing Humvees was too slow. So they decided to try a radically different approach. They took the busted ones apart, down to the last nut and bolt. Then they assembled new ones every sixteen minutes. And they were making them better. They put in the latest technology, better armor, and updated suspension systems. The Humvees come out better than they came in.

When I visited Red River for the first time, the plant could recreate thirty-two Humvees a day. When I checked in several months later, they were up to more than forty. From three a week to forty a day—that's a 6,600 percent improvement. Their flow time went down too, from forty days to ten days.

And what's amazing to me is that they didn't change any of the people working on the Humvees. They hired a few more, but basically the workers were the same union workers who had been there before. They changed the process, not the people. By changing how they worked, they unleashed a force that would have been unthinkable just a few years earlier. They changed what was possible for them to accomplish.

And they had pride, those workers. They put a sticker inside every Humvee: "We build it like our lives depend on it, because theirs do." And there was an 800 number, staffed twenty-four hours a day by volunteers who worked on the floor—not for money, but because it could be their brother or sister or cousin out there in a broken Humvee in the middle of a hostile land. Some of the workers had just returned from tours in Iraq or Afghanistan, and by God, they were going to help the army fix the vehicles they had built.

That night I called my father from the motel I was staying at in Texarkana. Remember, at this stage I was a reporter, not an expert in Scrum. "Dad," I said, "you know the Scrum and process-improvement thing I thought was a bunch of management garbage new-speak? Maybe I was wrong about that. Maybe you're on to something. Maybe."

So the Good Housekeeping pattern is about maintaining a clean product and a clean environment every single day. If anyone sees something wrong, you fix it, even if you didn't create the mistake yourself. Leave everything better than it was when you first touched it. In Toyota-speak, never pass on a known defect to the next station. If you have to test at the end for quality, your quality will be horrible; instead, build in quality every time you touch the product.

If you find yourself in this position, recognize that you can fix it. You can make these problems go away *forever*, just like the workers at Red River did. Change the way you are working and you will be amazed at what you are capable of.

Emergency Procedure

Problems arise in the middle of a Sprint due to emergent requirements or unanticipated changes. By mid-Sprint it may be obvious that the development team cannot complete the Sprint Backlog successfully. The team is high on the Sprint Burndown Chart and sees that they cannot achieve the Sprint Goal at the current rate of getting things done.

Therefore: When high on the burndown, try a technique used routinely by pilots. When bad things happen, execute an Emergency Procedure designed specifically for the problem.[9]

A Burndown Chart is a way of letting you see where the Team stands in the Sprint. You start with ten pieces of work in the Sprint, and each day you burn down how many pieces of work you got done. Let's say you are halfway through a Sprint. You look at the Team's burndown, and it's obvious there is no way the Team is going to get all that done—they've only gotten two things done. Their burndown just isn't going to get to zero by the end of the Sprint. It wasn't caused by interruptions; maybe the work is just harder than they thought, or they ran into unexpected problems. But the work ain't gonna happen—the plane is going down.

My father was a fighter pilot in Vietnam. He says that when bad things happen in a fighter plane, you immediately execute an emergency procedure. You could be dead before you can figure out what's going on. So there is a checklist attached to their left thigh, and they just start executing. No questions. In Scrum, the Scrum Master must execute a similar list immediately; it's just a rule.

Here's the checklist:

**EMERGENCY PROCEDURE STEPS
(DO ONLY AS MUCH AS NECESSARY)**

1. Change the way the work is done. Do something differently.
2. Get help, usually by offloading backlog to someone else.
3. Reduce scope.
4. Abort the Sprint and re-plan. Inform management how release dates will be affected.

Just roll down the list automatically. Because if you don't do anything, the whole Team is going down in flames. Pull up, pull up.

At 3M HIS, David said Tammy would pull up once in a while: "Tammy occasionally used the 'bat phone' to make a point—maybe half a dozen times." Tammy actually wishes her Teams would do it more often, so they don't sacrifice quality for speed. Use the "bat phone." It makes the problem visible. If Teams don't do it, you simply have no idea why dates keep slipping or quality starts to decrease. You have to encourage your Teams. Praise them for making you aware that an emergency is taking place.

Scrumming the Scrum

Only a small minority of Scrum teams make the paradigm shift to a radical new level of performance, and ability to create value. This is because most teams fail to identify and remove impediments.

Therefore: Identify the single most important impediment at the Sprint Retrospective and remove it before the end of the next Sprint.[10]

Scrum is designed to produce hyperproductive Teams. That's why the subtitle of our previous book refers to doing twice the work in half the time. That's not an exaggeration. That's the goal. With discipline, it is totally doable. But many Scrum Teams don't get that level of increase, and the cause is almost always the same: they fail to successfully identify and remove impediments.

It really is that simple. They're plenty busy, but they're not getting their work to done. And they accept that as the way the world is. Yes, that's the way the world *is* today in a lot of places. But it doesn't have to stay that way. This pattern is one way to get to done.

During each Sprint Retrospective, the Team should come up with one improvement—or *kaizen*, if you think Japanese sounds cooler. Just one. One impediment that they are going to get rid of in the course of that Sprint. Often they do identify an impediment, but then nothing happens. Everyone seems to think it is someone else's job to accomplish that, because they've got this huge backlog to get through.

My father was teaching a class on Scrum in Paris a while back, and a well-known Lean expert, Hugo Heitz, decided to take the class. During the course he kept coming up to my father and saying, "They need to put the *kaizen* in the backlog. They need to Scrum the Scrum. They need to use Scrum to make Scrum better."

After Jeff came back to Scrum Inc. he said, *We're going to try this. After we have our* kaizen, *as a Team we are going to estimate it and give it acceptance criteria, so we'll know when we are done, and we will put* it at the top of the backlog. *The* kaizen *will become the top priority for the next Sprint.* So we did. And within two or three Sprints our Velocity doubled. Furthermore, it kept on improving, and it continues to do so to this day.

Oftentimes I'll run across people inside a company who are just nihilists: "This place sucks! It sucks today. It'll suck tomorrow. It'll suck forever!" When I sit down and talk to them, that attitude usually stems from the fact that everyone knows what the problems are but nobody is fixing them. How demoralizing is that? The problems are known, maybe even the solutions are known, but no one does anything about them.

I'll go to management and tell them this. And they say, *We know. But we can't fix it because of* x, y, *or* z.

I'll wait for an uncomfortably long time before responding. You can feel this silent tension rising. Then I'll look at them and say, *It doesn't have to be that way, you know. It's a choice. Things can actually get better.*

At times those words sink in and they start actually fixing some problems, removing the stuff that is getting in the Team's way. It doesn't happen every time. I can't make them do it. But when they do, that nihilist becomes the greatest proponent of Scrum in the company, because stuff actually got fixed—finally.

At 3M they still do this, every single week. "It's probably given us more advancement than anything else. The Teams are constantly improving. And with one-week Sprints they're doing it fifty times a year," Tammy tells me. The improvements can be big and take a while to address, or maybe they're beyond the Team's sphere of influence, but it is that change in mindset, from accepting problems to actively seeking them out, that makes all the difference. Problems love to hide. They're like cockroaches in the walls. Pull them into the light. You'll be amazed—eradicating them won't be as scary as you think.

The Happiness Metric

In reflection and other self-improvement activities, there are generally many ideas for improvement. But you often don't know in advance which improvement activities will produce the greatest benefits, and which will not.

Therefore: Drive the improvement process with a single, small improvement at a time, chosen through team consensus. Pose a question to the team that helps them reflect on which of the alternatives on the table will best tap into their collective passion or sense of engagement, and use the answer to choose the improvement that will most energize the team.[11]

In *Scrum: The Art of Doing Twice the Work in Half the Time* we spend a whole chapter on happiness—Chapter 7, if you're interested. So I'm not going to spend a whole lot of time trying to convince you that morale is important. Trust me. It is. Dramatically. If people in your organization aren't happy and excited to work there, you've got a major problem on your hands. Happy people make better stuff faster. It's that simple.

The weird thing about happiness, though, is that it is the cause of success rather than the result of it. People base today's happiness on how they think the world will be next week, not how it was last week. If you put a quantifiable number on it, you have a leading indicator rather than a lagging indicator.

What you do is this. Every Retrospective, ask the Team publicly how happy they are in their role, how happy they are with their Team, and how happy they are with the company, on a scale from 1 to 5. And is there anything they can think of that would make them happier? That's it. It's pretty simple. I find it remarkable that every Team will focus in on the least happy person and say, *In the next Sprint, let's fix that.*

When Scrum Inc. introduced this, the first issue was better office space. People hated the current space. So we got a better space. Then it was better backlog items from the Product Owner. That one returned a couple of times in a row. And we just kept chipping away at the problems, one at a time, Sprint after Sprint. Soon enough our Velocity doubled, and doubled again. Twice the work. Half the time.

Talking the Talk Helps Walking the Walk

These eight patterns are the secret of doing Scrum well.

The first two, **Stable Teams** and **Yesterday's Weather**, set up the Team for a successful Sprint. If you can't do those, implementing Scrum just got a whole lot harder.

The next four, **Swarming, Interrupt Buffer, Emergency Procedure**, and **Good Housekeeping**, will help with the most common problems Teams have during a Sprint.

The final two, **Scrumming the Scrum** and **Happiness**, are the keys to continuous improvement at a sustainable pace. They are the ones that will move you into hyperproductivity—the design goal of Scrum.

And then the ninth pattern will emerge from the faithful execution of the others—**Teams That Finish Early Accelerate Faster.**

As Tammy Sparrow admits, it isn't perfect at 3M HIS. They still have a ways to go. But they have come far. The most important thing, she emphasizes, is that the conversations are different from what they used to be. The transparency of the whole system allows them to see where the hard problems are: the impact of organizational architecture, the issues around maintaining the legacy products that architecture produced. But now they seem fixable. She has changed what it is possible to do.

"If we get the backlog right," she says, "the Teams will soar."

I'm not saying it's easy. It *can* be. It can also be horribly difficult. But the way to make it easy is to be disciplined, and this requires focus and commitment. I hear sometimes that Agile is just for making people's lives better, happier. That's true; it does that. Or that Agile is really about building a great culture and company. Absolutely; that is accurate.

But it is all in service of something: the delivery of high value with alacrity. With speed. Speed matters. Speed in producing quality and speed in making decisions. The numbers are pretty stark: if you dally, your likelihood of success plummets.

So you'll have to make decisions based on imperfect and incomplete information. You'll have to move out into that fog of uncertainty. Because just like quantity, speed has a quality all its own.

All of these patterns interlock and reinforce each other. They are a pattern *language*. Start with one. Just one. The other words will come.

THE TAKEAWAY

Taxonomy of waste. This taxonomy divides waste into three categories: *muda*, "no result," or unfinished work; *mura*, "inconsistency or unevenness"; and *muri*, "no reason." This is the stuff that gets in the way of getting stuff done, such as overproduction, waiting, transportation, absurd expectations, and the like.

Kaizen. During each Sprint Retrospective, the Team should come up with one improvement, or *kaizen*, to try in the next Sprint. This could be removing an impediment, trying a different way of working, or anything else the Team feels will improve their speed. If the experiment pays off, keep doing it. If not (and not everything you try will work), throw it out.

Know the Scrum patterns.

- **Stable Teams** and **Yesterday's Weather** set up the Team for a successful Sprint. If you can't do those, implementing Scrum just got a whole lot harder.

- **Swarming, Interrupt Buffer, Emergency Procedure**, and **Good Housekeeping** will help with the most common problems Teams have during a Sprint.

- **Scrumming the Scrum** and **Happiness** are the keys to continuous improvement at a sustainable pace. They are the ones that will move you into hyperproductivity—the design goal of Scrum. Twice the work. Half the time.

- **Teams That Finish Early Accelerate Faster** is the pattern that will emerge from the faithful execution of the others.

BACKLOG

- Identify at least one instance of *mura*, *muda*, and *muri* in your workplace. How would you fix them?

- Create a Burndown Chart and start tracking your Team's progress during the Sprint.

- Implement each of the patterns described in this chapter. How did they affect the Team's Happiness and Velocity metrics? Did they change the slope of your Burndown Chart?

CHAPTER 8

What Not to Do

The existence of patterns, of course, implies that there are ways not to do things, or anti-patterns. Not every Scrum implementation works. They can fail. The interesting part is that when they fail, they often fail for the same reasons.

Again, Scrum is designed to bring problems to light quickly. Often that can be painful. And sometimes that pain makes it impossible for organizations to change.

A couple of years ago, soon after Kim Antelo started at Scrum Inc., she called me up after visiting a large automotive company we were working with. The client wasn't doing well. The people in charge had no power, there was endless backbiting and bickering, and they seemed to want to spend months and months arguing over what they should do, but not actually doing anything at all. I'll never forget that phone call.

"You're going to hate me, J.J."

"Why?"

"It's not going to work."

And then she began to tell me about the things that would stand in the way of the company becoming an Agile enterprise, and all the reasons those things were highly unlikely to change.

She was right.

So Scrum Inc. ended our relationship with that company. We can't make you do it. We can only help.

For years, I've been keeping a list of problems like this that show up over and over again at companies. I've found that knowing what not to do is as important as knowing what to do. Here are those anti-patterns and their countermeasures.

What Leaders Do
Don't Go Halfway

The needed organizational changes for the practice of Scrum are great. There will be different HR practices, a different reporting structure, different roles. To drive that reality through the organization, you need to have strong leadership at the C-level, because if you don't build a new way of doing things that becomes the way your company works, things can fall apart at the drop of a hat. You wind up with something that's not Agile but fragile instead.

Let me give you a personal example. The last company my father worked at before he founded Scrum Inc. was called PatientKeeper. They made handheld devices for doctors and hospitals. On a mobile device the medical staff could do everything—prescribe a medicine, order lab tests, see the test results, and so on. The administration liked it because it also allowed them to collect financial data, charge for services, and submit insurance claims.

At PatientKeeper my father was CTO. He met with the CEO

and talked about how he was going to run it with Scrum. "Fine," the CEO said, "but I'm tired of teams telling me things are 'done.' The only 'done' that matters is a payment from the hospital and no outstanding issues."

They spent the next two years building the capability to do that. They eventually brought multiple hospitals live each and every Sprint. Nowadays the ability to do that is a practice known as DevOps, and the tools are open-source and in the cloud. But back then they had to build the technology from scratch.

Once that was done, the CEO said that now they could change their priorities each week. Every Monday afternoon he would get the Product Owners and Scrum Masters together to review where they were on delivery, change anything that needed changing, fund anything that needed funding, and retarget the customers or competitors that were causing trouble. People said the CEO was like the Scrum Master of the Product Owner Team. He let the Chief Product Owner lead it, intervening only to remove impediments that same day—including changing management if that was the problem. My father says it was like an old English man-o'-war. Each week the POs would move the cannons around to fire on the enemy. The next week, another target. Within a year Patient-Keeper had no competition left. A lot of their work became uninstalling their competitors' products at hospital after hospital. Revenue jumped 400 percent in a year.

My father then decided to focus full-time on training people how to do Scrum and founded Scrum Inc. The person he left in charge had the Teams bringing up new hospitals every Sprint, like clockwork. A couple of years later that person left and the CEO hired a new head of engineering who did not understand Scrum. Within a month they couldn't deliver. The CEO told the new guy, *Do that again and you're fired.* It happened again. Then the CEO decided to take over the department himself, and reinstalled waterfall. Deliveries became long and painful. Revenue fell by half. PatientKeeper limped along for a few more years, but it's a great example of a great company being ruined with old practices.

The reason, Jeff thinks, is not only that the new people didn't understand Scrum, but they also didn't understand how the organization needed to constantly improve to maintain their pace. He saw it a year before they collapsed and warned them to fix it. But the management just expected Scrum to keep working, and if it didn't, it wasn't their fault. It was those engineers. And then, of course, the engineers started to leave.

I've seen that happen a few times. One executive puts something new into a business unit or even throughout a whole company, but they don't have the support from the top. And once they get promoted to another division or leave to join another company, the new way of working falls apart. Leadership is often shocked by this. How can they have the same people making the same thing, and all of a sudden their way of working just stops working? It happens because they haven't internalized the shift to Scrum, either for the organization or for themselves. The people they are leading, though, are rarely surprised by the winds of management change—they've blown through before.

The most effective Scrum implementations are those in which top leadership changes itself. They go all in. They publicly, financially, and operationally turn their organization into one that can operate in this new age of accelerating change. Scrum has to become the default way you get work done, from top to bottom. Iterate on what you are doing, not how you do it. If how you do it changes each time a new director walks in the door, you haven't really changed, you've only pretended to.

It's Not for Me, It's for Them

Scrum often begins in a single department—usually a place with a problem, often a serious one. They begin to go faster. And people notice. *Problem solved,* leadership thinks. *Awesome.* But other parts of the business don't change. They continually lob requirements and orders and projects like grenades over the cubicle walls, without regard to the damage they are doing. They don't consider whether the work should actually be done, how important it is in relation to other things people are working on, or if it can be done at all. You should think it through before you pull the pin.

What has to happen is that the rest of the organization, including leadership, needs to change their way of thinking about how they work, too. One of the big oil companies we worked with was replacing their whole safety reporting infrastructure a few years back. It was a big deal. They'd been trying to do it for years, and project after project had failed. Finally, they were able to convince two really ambitious executives from different parts of the organization to give it one more go. It was critical that it get done, and these two saw it as the opportunity it was. *Fix this big hairy problem, and the world is our oyster.*

One of them was given a copy of *Scrum: The Art of Doing Twice the Work in Half the Time* and was convinced it was the only way they could actually pull it off. Some Scrum Inc. colleagues and I flew in, trained their people, and launched a bunch of Scrum Teams. Things started to go really well, really quickly. But it kept running into a sticking point: the company's other leader. While she loved the results she was getting, she couldn't quite wrap her head around the idea that she needed to change her own behavior. So she continued to manage the group the same way she'd managed groups in the past.

Scrum is great at revealing problems. Soon enough it became clear that her decision-making was a problem. It was slowing the

Teams down. What surprised me was that it eventually became clear to her, and she did change. But it took making the problem and the cost of her behavior visible.

Ultimately, they launched on time, and everyone got a promotion. The other leader, the one who invited us to work with them in the first place, used that success to go back to her bosses and argue that Scrum shouldn't just be used with software projects—it should be used in all projects, whether digging a well, setting up an oil rig, or pumping oil through a pipeline. Scrum would give them such an advantage that they had to do it. So they are.

The first thing she did, though, was make sure that the leaders themselves understood how they would have to change.

Organizational Debt
Don't Lean Too Far

Lean principles are fantastic. Basically, they are the Western translation of the principles of the Toyota Production System: eliminate each and every piece of waste from the system. The Lean Enterprise Institute lists them this way:

1. Specify value from the standpoint of the end customer by product family.

2. Identify all the steps in the value stream for each product family, eliminating whenever possible those steps that do not create value.

3. Make the value-creating steps occur in tight sequence so the product will flow smoothly toward the customer.

4. As flow is introduced, let customers pull value from the next upstream activity.

5. As value is specified, value streams are identified, wasted steps are removed, and flow and pull are intro-

duced; begin the process again and continue it until a state of perfection is reached in which perfect value is created with no waste.

When it's correctly applied, Leaning out your enterprise will dramatically increase value delivery and remove the waste that slows it down.

The problem is that if you Lean things out too much, you can radically diminish your ability to innovate. A few companies I've seen have become incredibly fast at producing one thing with the fewest number of people needed. It's impressive. But there is no room for doing anything else *except* producing what they are producing now.

They concentrate on *kaizen*, those incremental changes that improve a system or a Team. Continuous improvement. Which is great, but they only focus on the current process, the current way of doing things. They aren't considering whether it is still the right way of doing things, or the right thing to do at all. A key aspect of the Toyota Production System is *kaikaku*, or radical change. It allows for shifting the whole business: new products, new strategies, new tools. It can be done in response to forces moving in the marketplace, like when the iPhone was introduced and everyone suddenly had to have smartphones rather than just phones. But it can also be driven internally. Usually with the incremental change of *kaizen*, those small steps level off. They no longer are improving things that much. So you implement a project to change *everything*— create a blank slate, start with a clean sheet, whatever you want to call it. You are looking for radical improvement.

But if you are too Lean, if you've downsized to just enough, there is absolutely no slack, and you just don't have time or the resources to innovate. One company I know became the single supplier of a key component in the iPhone. They made millions off it. But then Apple wanted something different that required a completely new approach. And because the supplier had made their system so Lean, it took them months to come up with that radical approach. You know what? Apple went with a different supplier who was able to move faster.

A Lean company is great, but if you take it too far, you end up with a company incapable of change.

Working the Way the Tools Tell You

There are a lot of Scrum tools out there. Software that manages your backlog and tracks your progress. I get pitched a new one at least once a week. I've used four different ones myself over the years. Each tool has its own quirks. Some want you to estimate how many hours each task will take. Some include reporting, but not the kind of reporting you want. Or they require a clumsy interaction with the system to get it to work. Or you have to check this box on five different screens to get what you want.

I see Teams tie themselves into knots trying to do Scrum the way the tool tells them to, even if what the tool requires is ridiculous in their circumstances. The tool was built with a certain way of working in mind. Most likely, what you need is different.

Here's what to do. I realize you are probably going to have to use some tool, but before you use it, put some Post-its on the wall for a couple of Sprints and figure out how your particular Team works best. It could be something as simple as how you indicate something is ready to be shown to the Product Owner. Or are there dependencies based on the work of other Teams that you need to make visible in some way, so that they know when they're holding you up?

Only after you've done that do you turn to the tool. Then you make the tool work the way you work, ignoring some features and using others in ways they might not have been intended to be used, but which work better for your Team. Make the robots work for you. Skynet, you've been warned.

How You Do It Matters
Cargo Cult Scrum

The island nation of Vanuatu, made up of roughly eighty islands, is famous for a few reasons. It was one of the first nations to be impacted by rising sea levels. It was the place that James Michener described in his 1947 book *Tales of the South Pacific*, which inspired Rodgers and Hammerstein to write the musical *South Pacific*. One of those scores of islands sprawled across some eight hundred miles of sea is Tanna. And on Tanna, February 15 is John Frum Day. John Frum is the messiah who will come and save them all with riches in the form of cargo. Stay with me here.

Before World War II, this island nation, then known as the New Hebrides, was one of those places that really didn't matter in the grand scheme of things. Until suddenly it did. The global conflict made these tiny islands quite important. The U.S. Navy arrived, and the Seabees cut roads through the jungle and built airfields and bases and barracks. Eventually some four hundred thousand troops were stationed there. And with them they brought cargo—hundreds of thousands of tons of supplies and matériel that washed over the island nation like a tsunami of abundance. Thus the figure of John Frum was born: "I'm John from America, want a candy bar?"

Then the war ended and the Americans left, abandoning their bases and airfields and taking with them the seemingly endless stream of goods that landed at airstrips or were offloaded at piers. John Frum was absorbed into the local religion, becoming the messiah who would bring the cargo back. To summon John Frum, the islanders would build replica airstrips in the jungle, with lights and a tower made from wood or branches or whatever local material they could scrounge up. The islanders believed that if they performed this ritual fervently and correctly enough, John Frum would return. I am totally not making this up.

Today, they still paint "USA" on their chests and dance an imitation of a military formation with wooden guns. John Frum will return, they proclaim. They even have a political party. Heck, one believer was ambassador to Russia briefly not that long ago. Cargo cults were, and are, quite real.

This kind of ritualization can happen around Scrum too. I've seen it. People go through the motions, treat the Scrum Guide as holy writ, and seem to believe the only purpose of Scrum is Scrum itself. I walk around "Scrum rooms" that are colorful and brightly lit and seem like fun until I ask if the Teams are delivering every Sprint. Then everyone gets a little uncomfortable.

At one of our large clients, a company with roughly fifty thousand employees and about seventy million customers, they had decided that since they were going to do Scrum, they would take all those people who had been project managers in the project management office and make them Scrum Masters.

With the true belief and fervor of the newly converted, those converted project managers embraced Scrum a little too hard and made it weird. They went to classes, they read the books, they went to conferences, they learned how to play Agile games, they talked a lot about what it really means to be a servant leader. And they went to work. They ran events. They used Post-it notes by the pallet. Like those praying for the return of John Frum, they mistook ritual and pantomime for action.

And no one listened to these new Scrum Masters. In meetings, they were roundly ignored. Their advice fell on deaf ears. They were seen as useless appendages, taking up time and space and money with no result.

The reason this happened is that their job description, quite literally, only read, "Facilitate Scrum events." That's it. There were no expectations they would do anything else. They were admins who ran meetings. None of them got the why of Scrum, only the how.

They didn't seem to grasp that Scrum is a way to get things done. Yes, people's lives will be better; hopefully they'll treat each other with respect; I'd hope work would be more fun. But as I said earlier, the sole reason a Scrum Master exists is speed. And that was lost on them.

"You have to be an expert on your Team," is what Scrum Inc.'s McCaul Baggett told me when I asked him how to fix Cargo Cult Scrum. McCaul is a coach and a trainer and the person I call on when a client's Scrum Masters need help.

"To be a successful Scrum Master," he said, "you have to be constantly communicating. That's the easy answer, but it's more complicated than that."

What you have to communicate to your Team is how they are doing, how they are performing, using data, said McCaul. If a Team isn't improving, you have to show them their Velocity, their Sprint commitments, how they are working, and ask them how they think they can improve. You have to watch every single *kaizen* that they come up with, and reflect back to your Team and ask, "Hey, is this working or not?"

Scrum Masters also have to look at how conversations are going. McCaul says it is a very different mindset than that of a Team Member or a Product Owner. A good Scrum Master isn't looking at whether the Team is talking about the right thing, but rather whether they are talking about the thing right. Because that makes things go faster.

Here's how he judges Scrum Masters: Is the Team constantly improving? Is the Team happy? That's the baseline. And are they improving the company? The last one is easy if they are removing impediments that are getting in the Team's way. The nature of their work removing what is slowing the Team down will not only affect their Team, it will likely help many Teams, and the company itself.

Don't just go through the motions. Ritual is not reality.

Don't Do A La Carte Scrum

Scrum is pretty simple—three roles, five events, three artifacts, five values. They are all important. And to get the radical change in productivity you are striving for, you have to have all of them. They are interlocking and reinforcing. Too often we see Teams that are missing one or more of them or are doing them poorly.

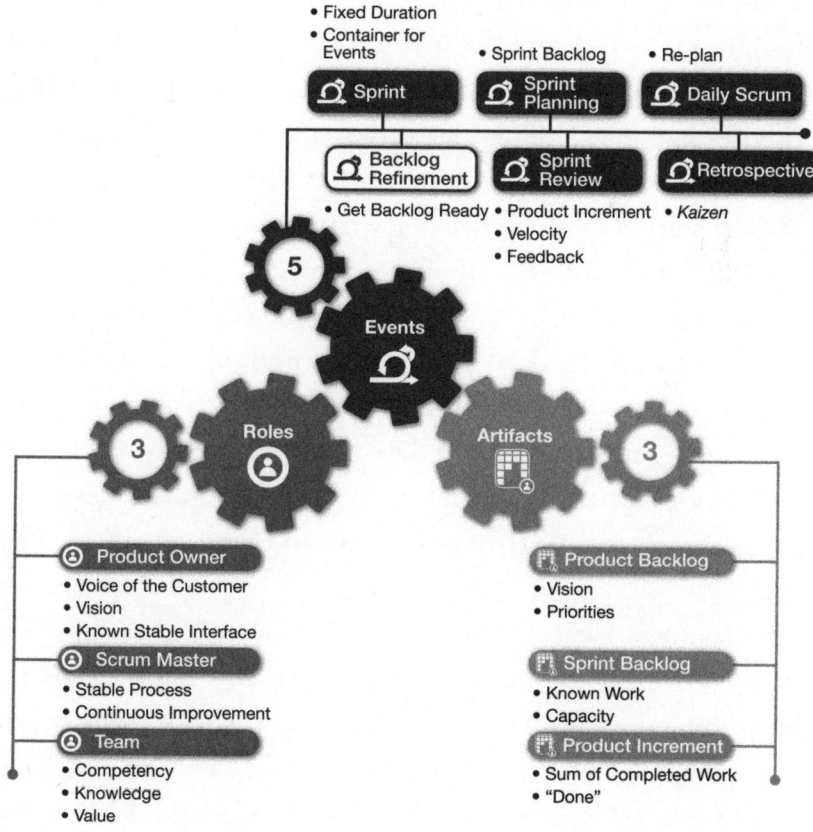

When Scrum Inc. is asked to evaluate a Scrum implementation, or to set one up, this is what we look at. All too often we see a Team, or many Teams, not having dedicated Team Members or a full-time Product Owner, or some other basic element. We like to set up a visible table of all the Teams and how (and how well) each element of Scrum is being implemented.

We usually put this on a whiteboard somewhere so the state of each Team is easy to see. On each aspect of the framework we indicate how they're doing. Are they doing well? Are they improving? Are things going downhill?

By simply checking this with each of your Teams, you can get a quick read on the state of Scrum in your company. It also makes the impediments to Scrum visible. Your Scrum Masters can use it as the basis of their prioritized impediment list. It's good to do this every Sprint. Or even after each event, as you are getting going. It doesn't take that long. By making it visible you can take action quickly, rather than finding out three months later that a Team won't deliver on time because they don't have good backlog because they started skipping Backlog Refinement.

Now, you may not have all of these elements in great shape all the time. That's okay. Start where you are, and work to slowly improve bit by bit. Heck, if you can only pull off a Daily Scrum, that alone will begin to make things visible and is going to help. And then you can start tackling the other pieces one by one.

But they all matter. They all have an impact. And it takes discipline and focus, constantly monitoring and tweaking and experimenting.

At a leading global agricultural equipment manufacturer they did this quite elegantly. At the beginning of their implementation of Scrum practices, they only did a few of the events. They began with a Daily Scrum. Then they added Sprint Planning and later Sprint Review. The person who had been tasked with leading the transformation of the group, eight R&D centers in multiple countries, didn't bang his fist on the table. He just kept sending emails each week about the advantage of this practice or that, this pattern or that one. The change was slow, incremental. But within eighteen months they had accelerated eightfold. More important, they were bringing their prototypes to market far more rapidly. They delivered real value by eventually doing Scrum properly, but they got there a day at a time.

Don't Outsource Competence

Most large organizations we work with do a huge amount of outsourcing. In some companies, contractors make up a majority of their workforce. I think that's completely crazy, by the way. But let's focus on the Scrum part of that practice. It is not uncommon for someone to call up and say, *Hey, can you get me fifty Scrum Masters who can start tomorrow?*

I suppose I could, and I'd make a lot of money that way. But I think it is a really bad idea to outsource a core competency like Scrum. If you want to truly make yourself into a Renaissance Enterprise, Scrum will become key in how you do what you do. If you outsource how to do it, you don't internalize the knowledge.

I'm not saying you shouldn't sign up for training and coaching—you'll probably need some of that. But make sure you have your own people getting training as well. You want the ability to do Scrum yourselves. At Scrum Inc. we believe in building truly great companies that can onboard, coach, maintain, and accelerate their own Teams. Our job is to build that capability within so you don't need us. I tell all our coaches and consultants that our job is to leave permanent change behind us. But, most important, to leave.

Scrum is a pretty simple framework, but it looks very different at an oil and gas company than it does at a bank or a research lab.

There are commonalities, of course, but every organization, like every Team, has its own culture and ways of thinking and doing. One size does not fit all.

Don't rent the talent that is going to make your organization great. Build it. Make it a part of everything you do.

Festering Impediments

A couple of years back I was in Silicon Valley visiting some of the new giants of technology, social media, and the Internet. I gave a talk at one of those tech giants and then asked the room, *What's your biggest impediment? What's slowing you down the most? What's getting in your way that is just maddening?*

One brave soul stood up and said, *There is a queue building up in front of deployment. It's eight days now. And it is growing. Instead of fixing the bottleneck in delivery, we're told only to build more features.*

I asked the room if that was true. Most of them nodded. A few clapped.

I asked the Scrum Masters in the room if they had made the problem visible to management. They had, they reported—but they'd been told to be quiet.

Six months later this big famous company (which I can't name because they made me sign an NDA to get into the building) fired their CEO, because things weren't getting delivered fast enough.

Often it is easy to see a problem. But sometimes it can be hard to fix. And sometimes it will take a long time to fix a really hairy one. Nevertheless, you have to start doing something to address it. If you don't, your people will know you're not taking their problems seriously.

What I encourage leadership teams to do is to have a visible impediments board. It should be located in a prominent, well-trafficked place. The outside of the CEO's doorway isn't a bad spot. And on that board should be the impediments that have been raised to that level, a picture of the manager whose responsibility it is to fix each one, and some way of showing how many days have passed from raising the impediment to resolving the impediment. If you can't get it on the CEO's door, track it yourself.

One time an old friend called me up. He was working on a major journalism project across the country with dozens of reporters and editors, and he was stuck. In fact, the whole project was stuck. They needed approvals for some things, and the approvals just weren't happening. The VP was busy. Or did not reply to email. Or said, *Tell the Scrum Master I'll get to it soon, but I have this really important meeting I have to be in right now.*

I told my friend to use Post-its to get up on a wall all the work that had to get done, and the board would reveal how this one Post-it note not moving was blocking all the other work. Then take out his phone and take a picture and mail it not only to the VP but to all of the other VPs as well. Be nice. Be polite. But do it every single day—*Hey, just making sure you know we're still blocked, really appreciate your help on this, totally understand your busy schedule.* Took three days for the problem to go away.

Fix the problems that arise. Or at least begin to fix them. Show people what you're doing to fix them. In doing so you will have shown very clearly your commitment to becoming a Scrum company.

Focus on What Works
You Live or Die by Product Owners

Product Owners are the known stable interface between the Team and the rest of the world. They are responsible for a heck of a lot, and are accountable for a heck of a lot. They are the ones deciding what the market needs and in what order and how fast the Team can deliver it.

But what happens is that sometimes the job is seen as unimportant. Or the company changes the job title from Business Analyst to Product Owner but does not change the job description—nothing has changed but nomenclature. Or the company takes an incredibly busy manager and says, *Hey, you're a Product Owner now too. But continue doing your old job.* Or an executive insists on being a Product Owner but doesn't have the time to interact with the Team. Or you've made a senior technical person a Product Owner and they don't communicate that much with stakeholders or customers. If you keep doing things the same way you always have, you'll get the results you always did before. Good Product Owners are the key to winning with Scrum.

The Chief Product Owner of Scrum Inc., Patrick Roach, describes it this way: "You're leading an expedition into the unknown and success will be determined by your game plan. Survival is dependent on your ability to inspire creativity in those around you when, inevitably, shit hits the fan. It's an exhilarating role with serious consequences." Serious consequences indeed.

One of the saddest things I've ever seen is having really good people doing really incredible work, really fast, but making the wrong thing. Or making the thing wrong. Let me give you two examples. Nokia Mobile went from industry dominance to complete irrelevance in just a few years. And they had really good Scrum Teams. Fast ones. There was even the Nokia Test to see if you were really Agile or not, featuring questions like *How long are your Sprints? Do you have a Product Owner? Do you have a Burndown Chart? Do you have a prioritized backlog?*

But like any test, it can be misleading if all you are doing is checking the boxes. Nokia had really good Scrum Teams delivering incredibly quickly. Of course, after the introduction of the iPhone, those really good Scrum Teams were incredibly quickly delivering the *wrong thing*! And that is because the Product Owners didn't react fast enough to a major shift in the market. Nokia's failure wasn't the fault of the Teams; it was the fault of the Product Owners.

As another example, I worked with a financial services firm to help them completely rebuild their transaction systems in the cloud. They wanted to be able to update their fraud protection as criminals updated the ways they were committing fraud. And the criminals were doing it faster than they were. It was pretty high stakes, because they had millions of customers and many millions of transactions a day, and if this thing wasn't launched on a particular date that summer, they would have to pay a third-party vendor an absurdly large sum of money to handle those transactions for them. Tens of millions of dollars.

The real key to driving that project's success was a brilliant group of Product Owners who were laser-focused on getting the right backlog at the right time. They allowed no off-backlog work. The Product Owners were held accountable each and every Sprint. They would occasionally send me their Burndown Chart for the whole project. It sloped almost perfectly to the date they had to hit. And they hit it. By Black Friday they were completely on the new system: 600 transactions a second, 50-millisecond response time, 99.9 percent uptime. And now they can change their fraud model seamlessly. It's saving them $38 million a year. And that vendor, yeah, they turned that off, saving another $40 million a year. That's the kind of thing a great Product Owner can do.

A great Product Owner can fundamentally change an organization's trajectory. Remember, a Product Owner has to be decisive, able to make decisions quickly based on incomplete information. They have to be knowledgeable; they have to know enough about the domain and the market to make informed decisions. They have to be available both to the Team and to the customer, a 50/50 split of their time being a good rule of thumb; if they can't do that, they might be a stakeholder, but not a Product Owner. They have to be empowered to act, with the freedom and power to make good decisions and get backup from leadership when they do that. Finally, they have to be accountable, since they are on the hook for the success of whatever it is their Team is doing.

Know What Does and Doesn't Have to Happen

Dave Slaten is one of our Product Owner whisperers at Scrum Inc. One of those soft-spoken and fierce people. He has seen many organizations die from poor Product Ownership, so he's developed a tool kit to help fix that. The part I want to share with you here is what I consider the most important part of being a Product Owner: what not to do.

Dave runs an exercise he calls the alignment map. I call it a wall of pain. Dave begins it by having the Product Owners leave the room (they're only supposed to spend 50 percent of their time with the Team, after all) and write down the most important things they want the Teams to be working on. Once the POs have left, he has the Team Members write down what they are actually working on. Eventually he reunites the POs and the Teams and has them compare what they've written down. The vast majority of the time, says Dave, the Teams are working on some of the top-priority stuff. But there is a significant part of what they are doing that is low priority. Things no one actually wants.

The fix, notes Dave, is simple. Teach the Product Owners to think of backlog items in a different way. They need to make clear what is needed at this particular time, what Dave calls the minimum delivery. When backlog items are written correctly, what the PO and Team Members write down will align perfectly. This exercise drives that by emphasizing the need for good acceptance criteria specifically written to answer a simple question: "I know this is done when . . ."

As Dave explains, well-crafted acceptance criteria "don't tell the Team what they have to make happen" but make clear to the Team "all the stuff that they don't have to make happen." Deciding what not to do is far more important than deciding what to do. Only build what is needed right now. This Sprint. Not the whole thing at once.

Data Doesn't Care About Your Opinion

One of the weirdest moments I've ever experienced in business took place in a nondescript office park, the kind of place where you wonder if the architects take special pride in their ability to achieve the epitome of bland.

Anyway, inside this bland building was a bland conference room, remarkable only for its size. It was big. It held thirty or forty executives at a huge U-shaped table. This was their annual planning meeting to decide what projects they were going to do in the next year. I was interested in seeing how they did it.

One of the senior vice presidents projected a spreadsheet onto the wall with a bunch of projects. Not really prioritized, just stuff they felt they had to do. The "big rocks," as they called them. The senior VP looked around the room; everyone had stacks of paper and laptops open to other spreadsheets, with their assistants whispering in their ear occasionally. He said, "Okay, we've got five hundred thousand personnel hours over the next year. That's including employees and contractors. So, Sarah, you've got the first item on this list. How many hours do you think you'll need?"

Sarah consulted her papers and laptop and assistant. "Twenty-five thousand hours."

Another VP piped up, "Is that enough? It's tricky."

"Okay, make it thirty-five thousand."

And so it went. There was no rationale offered for the numbers given. No sense of any estimates beyond the wild guesses being made in the room. In the previous year, by the way, they had gotten exactly *one* of their twelve big rocks done.

I knew that as soon as this meeting broke up, Sarah's Teams—however many people thirty-five thousand hours makes up, and they were probably on different Teams spread around the planet—were on the hook for delivering that first item on the list. There were budgets, requirements, and dates attached to those thirty-five thousand hours, no matter how accurate or inaccurate the estimate.

My colleague Joe Justice told me an even wilder story about a—let's call it a "unique"—way of decision-making on projects and budgets. He was working with a global manufacturer and got invited to the planning session for the coming year. It took place on a cruise ship. And yes, it turned out to be a booze cruise. "So these slightly drunk people were in a ballroom on a boat, drinking heavily while they decided the priorities for the next year, the budgets, and who was responsible for which project," Joe told me. "It was absolutely insane. There was no reasoning behind it. No logic. No data. Just a bunch of inebriated executives." And they were deciding how to spend hundreds of millions of dollars.

You know what? Both of those companies were probably doing the best that they could. Because they didn't have the right data.

Scrum creates massive amounts of data: Velocity, Process Efficiency, Happiness metrics, and more. But you have to use it. Know the Velocity of your Teams. Have the people that are going to do the work estimate the work. And then track the progress in real time, Sprint by Sprint. If it starts going off the rails, you will know it early on, so you can course-correct.

When Kim Antelo began working with a multinational manufacturing company, they were an incredibly siloed organization. Each vice president ran their piece of the business as their own fiefdom. This led to different parts of the company building the *exact* same thing independently, multiple times, and not telling anyone else about it. Their lack of priorities meant that when Kim started to work with the company's leadership she uncovered *two thousand* different products that were being worked on. That worked out to be about two for each and every employee.

To try to stop going down that path, they formed a Product Owner Team to really look at what they were doing. They were able to get it down to about two hundred products in twenty different product groups. The Product Owner Team at this level was really a bunch of Chief Chief Product Owners, each of whom had many Chief Product Owners in their groups, who each had a Product Owner Team of their own working with their Teams. (One group that did this had three levels of Chief Product Owners, and yes, the person at the top was commonly referred to as the C3PO.)

These Product Owners would come together once a week to see where things stood and talk about what had happened that would change their priorities. Once a quarter they would decide what would be funded further and what wouldn't. For each product they would do a deep dive, sharing their hypotheses, informed by the data flowing from their Scrum Teams, on what they thought they could deliver. They were funded only for that quarter. They had to come back a few months later and show what they had learned, what the next set of problems was that they were going to tackle, and when they thought they could get a product out the door. Only then would they get more funding.

Sometimes they learned that they really shouldn't be making something. Or that a product that they hadn't thought was important turned out to be *really* important. Because they did their funding iteratively, continuously throughout the course of a year, instead of determining all the project funding at the beginning of the year when they knew the least about what was going to happen, they could quickly turn the wheel if things started to go wrong. They could change their priorities at a very high level based on actual results rather than blind guesses. It made prioritization across the whole organization quite easy, because they used data rather than opinion to drive their decision-making.

Let me give you another example of what transparency can do for you. The CEO of a big data company we were working with had a few projects spread across a bunch of Teams. Dozens of them. And she wanted to know about their Velocity on a particular project, not the Velocity of the Teams, because of course they were working on a bunch of other stuff. The question was how quickly they were getting this particular project done.

That wasn't a problem, we told her. All she had to do was add up the estimates of the Teams. *But you can't compare Velocity and estimates across Teams,* the CEO said. *That's what you told us.* Sure, we told her, and what do we know about all estimates? They're wrong. All of them. In this case there were just enough Teams that we could aggregate the estimates, and the differences would come out in the wash.

They tagged the relevant backlog items with "Really Important Project." And then they got a burndown across multiple Teams, Sprint by Sprint. So she was able to see, each week, how fast the Teams were burning down this particular project.

For the sake of argument, let's say they were burning down twenty to twenty-five pieces of this Really Important Project every week for a few weeks. The burndown rate was looking great, and confidence was high that they would deliver on time. But an odd thing happened. As the CEO watched week by week, the numbers were good for a while, and then they dropped dramatically for a few Sprints. What was going on? After all, this was the CEO's priority. So we looked into it. It turned out that another executive had prioritized something else for those Teams, slowing their Velocity on the Really Important Project.

Because the CEO knew this months before the desired release date, she could take action and bend that curve back in the right direction. She felt for the first time that she could actually steer her organization and know the state of the things she cared about. She didn't need status reports or PowerPoint presentations that continually said the project was in the green until about two weeks before the deadline, when it would flip to red. She didn't need opinions or carefully crafted reports—she had *data*.

With Scrum, you get lots of data. You can experiment and see the results quickly. An empirical system is constantly inspecting and adapting: probe, response, evaluate, probe, response, evaluate. It's important you do this in real time both at the Team level and at the enterprise level. In a way, it's a safety net. You aren't risking hundreds of millions of dollars on a yearlong project; you're only doing it for a Sprint. And you can change your mind at any time as conditions change.

The great thing about how poorly most organizations are run is that it is easy to have a dramatic impact quickly. I've discussed some of these before, but I want to put them all in one place so they are easy to find. These are the things that will radically increase a Team's Velocity almost overnight.

- ☐ *Stable Teams.* Bring projects to people, not people to projects.
- ☐ *Yesterday's Weather.* Only commit to do what you did last time.
- ☐ *Dedicated Teams.* Context switching between Teams will kill you.

- ☐ *Daily Scrum.* Every day. Same time. Same place.
- ☐ *Interrupt Buffer.* Have a plan for the unexpected.
- ☐ *Small Teams.* Three to nine is the ideal. Larger and you will slow down dramatically.
- ☐ *Ready backlog.* Clarity on what needs to be done.
- ☐ *Good Housekeeping.* Don't let a known defect escape the day.
- ☐ *T-shaped people (enables Swarming).* Don't have a single point of failure.
- ☐ *Done done.* At the end of each Sprint the work is completely and totally done.
- ☐ *Collocation.* Everyone should be in earshot of each other.

If you don't have all of those, start with one. And bit by bit, Sprint by Sprint, *kaizen* by *kaizen*, move toward the goal of having them all. You may not be able to. There may be things that are simply outside of your control. That's okay.

How you do what you do matters. If you decide not to do something, you need to know the cost of the decision you are making. All too often that isn't visible. But you have to see the world for what it is. Because if you can't see it, if you can't talk about it, if you can't question it, you can't fix it.

And I want you to fix it, I really do. I want a world where people's full potential is unleashed. Once you make that shift from acceptance to action, from passive to powerful, the world you work in will never be the same. I want to live in a future where the waste of human potential is seen as the unnecessary and unneeded tragedy it truly is. I want to be amazed by what we are creating.

And you can do it. What you decide is a choice. The future is not fixed.

THE TAKEAWAY

Watch out for anti-patterns. Ever heard anyone say "I'm going to find a list of the worst practices and follow them"? Of course not. Not every Scrum implementation works. They can fail. The interesting part is that when they fail, they often fail for the same reasons.

The problem with à la carte Scrum. Yes, even bad or partial Scrum can boost productivity, but only so far. Scrum is pretty simple—three roles, five events, three artifacts, five values. They are all important. And to get the radical change in productivity you are striving for you have to have all of them. They are interlocking and reinforcing.

Leadership. The most effective Scrum implementations are those in which top leadership changes itself. They go all in. Scrum has to become the default way you get work done, from top to bottom. Because if you don't build a new way of doing things that becomes the way your company works, it can fall apart at the drop of a hat. It's not Agile, it's fragile.

Data, not opinions. Scrum creates massive amounts of data. But you have to use it. You can experiment and see the results quickly. An empirical system is constantly inspecting and adapting: probe, response, evaluate, probe, response, evaluate.

Don't outsource competence. Don't rent the talent that is going to make your organization great. Acquire it. Make it a part of everything you do. If you outsource how to do it, you don't internalize the knowledge.

BACKLOG

- Identify how many anti-patterns you or your organization currently practice. Write each on a Post-it note and place them on a wall. Remove the note only when you've removed the pattern.

CHAPTER 9

The Renaissance Enterprise

When Eric Abecassis became the CIO of Schlumberger in January 2017, he had one of those problems that can make or break a career. Schlumberger had already invested a considerable amount of money into a project that would impact the company's future: a critical modernization of their IT systems. Despite the resources they'd put in, the project was facing significant challenges.

He decided it was time to do something more radical. That's when he called in Scrum Inc. to help look for more agile ways of working. Abecassis explained his reasoning to Schlumberger executive management as follows: "The experiment with Scrum will only last a few months. But if we are successful, it's going to be a major breakthrough in terms of efficiency." The impact would be felt across the whole company, not just the back office. It could have the potential to radically affect how the company does things.

Birth of a Quiet Giant

Schlumberger is one of those companies—either you've never heard of it and mispronounce the name, or you're kind of startled by just how ubiquitous it is. Basically, if there is oil and gas being drilled somewhere on the planet, there's a pretty good chance that they are the ones doing it. They don't own the reservoirs—the big oil and gas companies do. What Schlumberger owns is the technology and expertise in how to do it. They deliver products and services in more than 120 countries and employ about 100,000 people of some 140 different nationalities.

The company was founded in 1926 by two brothers, Conrad and Marcel Schlumberger. What they did was invent something so basic to the oil and gas industry that it is pretty fair to say the size and scope of the industry would not be possible without it. They invented the technique known as electrical well logging. They created a device that could be lowered down the well on a cable, a probe known as a sonde, that detects the electrical resistance of the surrounding rock. By taking a reading at certain intervals and then logging the change in resistance as they probed the well bore, it became a lot easier to analyze the subsurface and find the oil.

As the demand for oil grew, so too did Schlumberger. They spent a lot of time and resources on research and development, staying at the very forefront of technology for the oil and gas industry. In 1981, they were the first company to send data links via email; they were among the first companies to use Arpanet, the precursor to the Internet. In 1991, Schlumberger evolved its private network, one of the largest in the world at the time, by using TCP/IP for an open architecture network to improve performance and increase interoperability.

Dealing with the Complexity of Growth

Like lots of large companies, Schlumberger acquired any number of smaller firms in the twentieth century. But integrating IT business systems from acquisitions is no easy task. Schlumberger realized it had 150 different legacy IT systems running on all sorts of different computers, with different operating systems, and no one could see the whole picture.

So, they decided to fix it. They'd get a grand system that linked all these existing systems, what's called an Enterprise Resource Planning system (ERP). These are like the capillaries of a modern multinational company. An enterprise system is supposed to link everything together—cash, raw materials, business processes, payroll, accounting, purchase orders, supply chain, you name it. They picked SAP, the dominant player in ERPs, and started in on making it work for Schlumberger, customizing features as they went. It was one big, complex project.

A little more than a year before being named CIO, Abecassis had been working on the SAP implementation. Even then it was a massive endeavor, involving six hundred people. "When I came back fifteen months later," Abecassis says, "it was not six hundred people, it was thirteen hundred people. It's impossible to have thirteen hundred people day in and day out being coordinated," says Abecassis.

Then he looked at the productivity numbers. They were producing exactly the same amount as they had before, with more than double the people. Adding people had changed nothing except the costs and increased the complexity of the organization.

"We desperately needed a breakthrough that would enable us to work more productively," says Abecassis.

Fixing the Fix

Scrum Inc. began working with the company just before Thanksgiving. The first few Sprints were rough—it wasn't easy. But, Jim Brady, the Vice President of IT architecture and governance, says that soon turned around. By May, productivity had jumped 25 percent. "It was a very fast change that had an impact. And we had reduced the number of external contractors by 40 percent. So, while it's not quite twice the work with half the people, we were clearly on that trajectory."

Abecassis says they've now reduced costs of the whole project by 25 percent already. And they're not done yet. "I think we can continue to push the envelope," he says. "We can definitely get to maybe 30 to 40 percent cost savings, and 30 to 40 percent of productivity improvement—we're on a very good track."

Their SAP implementation in North America, Schlumberger's largest market, went live in April 2019 as a fully working product. Just by changing how they were working.

A Different Way of Thinking

As the great management guru Peter Drucker put it, "Anything that contradicts what we have come to consider a law of nature is rejected as unsound, unhealthy, and obviously abnormal."[1] There will be resistance to change. There will. Even in the face of sure and utter destruction.

You have to expect that. You have to be ready for it. You have to have a plan. You need to internalize that once you take an action there will be friction and resistance. At Schlumberger, the change involved in adopting Scrum practices was challenging for some people.

Abecassis's plan to drive the change was to focus on converting those in his organization that could be converted. And once they saw the impact they could have and the opportunity to effect real change, they were all in.

As Scrum succeeded inside, it began to spread. Eventually, Eric's Leadership Team got together for a planning session. There was a sense of uncertainty: they weren't sure how to operate in this new way of working.

But it was like hitting bottom, says Abecassis. "From that point, they jumped back up and said, 'Okay we're going to make it.' And that created the momentum that resulted in an increase in our Team's productivity. But the main result is that we transformed my organization into one Team with one mission. That was the magic."

When you begin practicing Scrum, expect that resistance. There will be forces working against you. It could be something totally out of your control—the customer changes their mind, your competitors do something differently, new technology emerges. Or the challenges could be internal to your company—your people, manufacturing problems, the size of your budget.

A credit card company I was working with had that problem. The Teams were successful, so other groups started poaching Team Members, getting the best ones assigned to them. You can imagine the impact on the existing Teams and on company morale. You need to figure out a way to protect your Scrum Teams from the "institutional antibodies" that may try to attack them.

One common way to do this is to implement a dual operating system. On one side of a very bright line you have your Agile teams; on the other side you have your traditional hierarchy. The key is to set up clearly defined interfaces between the two.

Let me give you an example. Markem Imaje makes industrial

products for tracking, identifying, and labeling everything from cosmetics to candy to dairy products. A major part of their product line is industrial printers. Really high-speed printers, like the ones to print dates on food containers. The company has been in business for over a hundred years. For decades, every time they put out a new printer they had to set up a special call center and form a "tiger team" of experts to go out and quickly fix all the defects in the new generation of these industrial printers. It was a painful process. There were unhappy customers. The process was exhausting for the whole company. And it hurt financially too—after enough failed product releases, customers get a little less willing to buy your next one.

A few years back, Markem Imaje put together the Teams to make their next-generation printer: software, electromechanical, chemistry, marketing, sales, manufacturing, quality assurance. They created a little business unit. A guy named Chris Sullivan brought in Scrum Inc. to help transition the software Teams to a new way of working. He wanted high quality quickly, and he figured at least the software Teams would be accepting of Scrum. That piece of it worked. But the rest of the Teams didn't want to practice Scrum.

They didn't understand the benefits or didn't see any reason to change the way they had always worked. *Fine,* Chris told them. *But there is one thing I want you to do. I want fifteen minutes a day with representatives of each group—leaders, people who can change things. Only fifteen minutes. I want a Scaled Daily Scrum, so we can coordinate.* He says the process was really uncomfortable at first. People were reluctant to be open about problems they were having. But it had a huge impact. They were able to communicate quickly and drive down the time it took to make decisions—problems that once would have taken months to be made visible were resolved in hours. Things like, say, if the electromechanical people casually mentioned they were changing the nozzle shape slightly for some design reason, the chemistry people would say, "Thank God you told me that now. I'm going to have to change the viscosity of the ink."

As they got ready to release the new machine, Markem Imaje got nervous. *Here we go again,* management thought. They set up their tiger team. They staffed their special call center. The new printer was released. And they waited. And the phone didn't ring. For months. When it finally did, it was a happy customer wanting a minor enhancement.

For the first time in a hundred years they had had a zero-defect release. The person in charge of manufacturing at Markem Imaje told Chris later, "I was reluctant at first, but the Daily Scrum of Scrums was the key reason this is the best launch in our history."

Living the Change

I want to tell you a bit more about just one of the Teams at Schlumberger; they are responsible for converting the data from those 150 legacy systems in all the locations throughout North America. Their target was to have 70 percent of the legacy systems converted at every site. The most they had ever accomplished was 17 percent. You can imagine how happy management was.

When Scrum was implemented, they struggled with the same things many Teams do. They were geographically distributed, with Team Members in Texas, France, and India. They had limited access to subject matter experts (SMEs); one SME was expected to work on four different Scrum Teams at the same time. And they simply didn't have enough people. It was tough.

Alexandra Uriarte, a Scrum Inc. Coach and Trainer who worked with the Team for months, told me that the real keys were the Team's fully dedicated and full-time Scrum Master and Product Owner. The Product Owner, Walter, said that after being trained by Alex, they made a decision: "We really wanted to put into practice everything we learned in our training. We knew that how we were currently operating was not working."

They did what they could. They started out with one-week Sprints. To their surprise, the tighter feedback loop had a dramatic impact. In just seven Sprints they doubled their Velocity. They found that by keeping the work to small pieces that could be done in short periods of time, the whole Team was able to Swarm on them, working together to rapidly find problems and uncover solutions.

Alex checked in on the Team's morale every two weeks. The Scrum Master was using the Happiness metric in their review. Interestingly, says Alex, they found morale was a predictor not only of the amount of stuff they could get done but also of the *quality* of their work. The ups and downs and growing pains of the Team were reflected in their Happiness metric—when the metric went down, quantity and quality suffered, but when it bounced back, speed and performance did too.

They decided to co-locate where they could. Even if they couldn't all be together, the Team Members in Texas decided they would give it a go. At least part of the Team could try to sit together. Even though they were in the same building, they had still been sitting apart, using the cubicles they'd been assigned before being put on a Scrum Team together. Walter encouraged them to take over one large room so they could work side by side. Not surprisingly, it increased their Velocity.

And they tackled the eternal problem of overcommitting. They often pulled more work into a Sprint than they could possibly complete. To address that, they implemented the Yesterday's Weather pattern I wrote about in Chapter 8: only commit to the amount of work you actually finished in the last Sprint. Sure enough, it made them go faster. Instead of overcommitting, they started to overdeliver.

Nothing speaks louder than success. Alex says that what she calls the "teaminess" of the Team—trust, friendship, camaraderie—grew quickly, even as they expanded. And this Team, which had never delivered on time, delivered a week early. From 17 percent readiness, they improved to 93 percent. And they decided to help out two other countries outside of North America, doubling their readiness. *In their spare time!* They had become capable of doing things that would have seemed like a pipe dream a few months earlier. All in all, it took them about five months to deliver what they had never done before.

Again, when something isn't working, it's not the people, it's the process. You need to release the people to do what they are capable of. That capacity is there. You just have to let it out by getting out of the way.

Scrum@Scale

As Scrum Teams self-organize and distribute the work, a network of Teams does the same thing. As I discussed in Chapter 3, you want to push decisions out through the network to those nodes on the edge, so as you scale, you scale robustly. If one node goes down, it's not that big a deal. The system becomes self-healing, growing, responding, and changing as the environment does.

The key is to have a set of known stable interfaces between components of any part of the network. Think back to the Saab Gripen E Team. They created the interfaces between each piece of the plane to be stable but fixed, like Lego. They could pull pieces out in one place without affecting the rest of the plane at all. The

Saab Teams' organizational structure was similar, with each Team, or Team of Teams, responsible for one module—the radar folk over here, the engine folk over there, and the fuselage group over yonder. Just like the individual components of the plane have known stable interfaces, so too do the Teams themselves. It's Conway's law at work. Just as you want your products to be made up of loosely coupled components, you want your organization to be set up the same way. Reports, readouts, and updates sent from one level of the organization to another are waste. Any management is waste, really. In a perfect world, you'd have no management at all—there would only be Teams producing value. This is the real world, however, and you do need some structure, as I said in Chapter 6—but just enough, the minimum viable bureaucracy.

By having these known stable interfaces, you create a complex adaptive system that can learn and change as it grows. The "right" organization *emerges* through fast inspect and adapt cycles. Remember, though, the form of this organization will be different for different companies, because they are trying to do different things.

At Schlumberger, for example, their goal was pretty simple—reduce costs and deliver quickly. The goal of the Stealth Rocket Company I told you about was to get to space fast. In a start-up, money is important, but delivery is even more important to keep getting new money from investors. So they focused on innovation and agility.

Autodesk, which has about 85 percent market share of the computer-aided design market, wants to be more Agile. They want to move toward emergent design and adaptable processes, for two reasons. The first involves making Autodesk a place where people want to work, like Google or Saab. As their head of Agile told me a few years back, "Listen, our existential threat isn't a peer competitor, it's four guys in a garage who won't let us buy them."

So they want to make Autodesk a cool place to work. The second reason is that Autodesk is changing their whole business model. For years they depended on expensive upfront licenses for their products, like lots of software companies did. But then back in 2014, when they really started accelerating their Scrum adoption, they slipped this bland bit of corporate-speak onto page 40 of their annual report:

> Autodesk's business model is evolving. . . . Over time, we expect our business model transition to expand our customer base by eliminating higher upfront licensing costs and providing more flexibility with how customers use our products. However, we expect the business model transition to cause our traditional upfront perpetual license revenue to decline, without a corresponding decrease in expenses. In the future, we expect this business model transition will increase our long-term revenue growth rate by increasing the annual value per subscription and increasing our subscription base over time.

They were announcing they were moving away from making money from licenses and toward making money from subscriptions. The *en vogue* acronym for this is SAAS, Software As A Service. The idea is you create a "stickier" relationship with your customers. Autodesk started doing this—and they started losing money. Lots of money. But they kept at it. Then in 2016, investors caught on and started thinking it was a really good idea. Over the next two years, Autodesk's stock rose by 121 percent. Their price-to-earnings ratio went from $3.50 in 2013 to more than $13 in 2018.

That is a really big premium, far more than their competitors'.

And they were still *losing* money. In May 2018, the investment website The Motley Fool weighed in, saying investors aren't stupid—they are seeing the power of the shift in business model by the dominant player in their market:[2]

> And, finally, Autodesk's product—software—has the potential to become easier to deliver and to create a shorter feedback loop via the cloud between the end user and the company. This means the company can save on costs and get better at satisfying the desires of its customers.

As Michael Hammer and Lisa Hershman put it in their book of the same name: faster, cheaper, better.

All of these companies are now using Scrum—but they are using it to achieve different ends. That means their organizational architecture will look different too. There is no one-size-fits-all way of doing things. Instead, you have to help your organization emerge as you go. It's not random, of course—you want to have a starting point—but you simply can't do it all upfront. You set the initial conditions and then inspect and adapt. Organizations, like products, have to evolve quickly.

Beginning the Renaissance

The period of European history we call the Renaissance was named well after the fact by Jules Michelet in his masterwork *Histoire de France*, published in the mid-nineteenth century. The term *renaissance* literally translates from the French as "rebirth." And that is exactly how companies need to think. They need to be reborn as places that can do things quickly, learn quickly, and act quickly. To do Scrum@Scale, you need to separate out what you are doing from how you are doing it, just like an individual Scrum Team. Here's what it looks like:

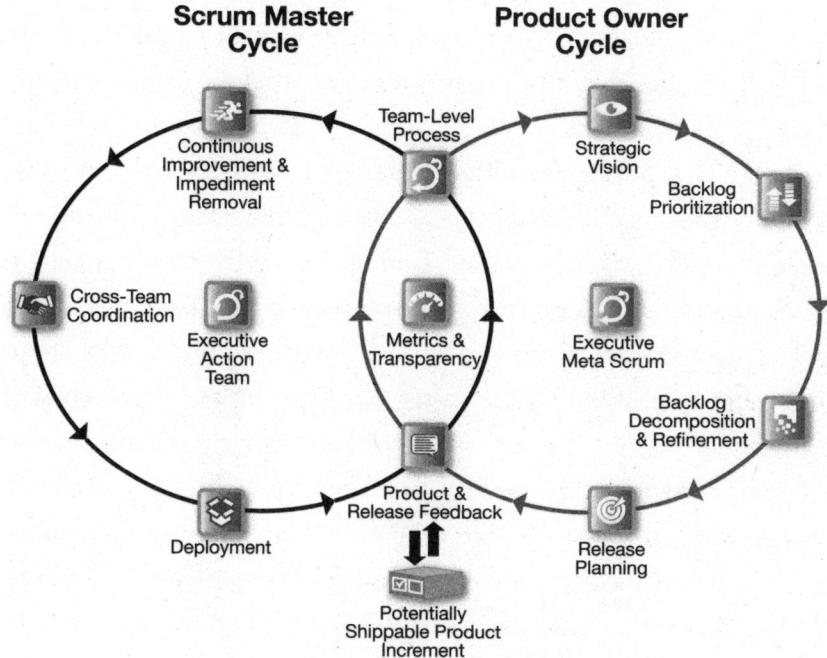

At Schlumberger they are using Scrum@Scale to spread Scrum across all the countries they operate in. "We're looking at a radical approach based on Scrum with a Scrum@Scale mechanism to make sure we have the proper control in the center, but radical autonomy at the country level," says Jim Brady. "That will allow us to speed up the deployment and actually capture even more net to the bottom line."

The Scrum Master Cycle

On one side you have the Scrum Master cycle. It revolves around the Executive Action Team, the leadership group that I wrote about in Chapter 6. The Scrum Masters at the Team level focus on continuous improvement, both in their Teams and in the Teams they have to coordinate with, identifying dependencies and figuring out how they are going to get a product out the door together. They are responsible for making everything visible, both successes and failures, so that the organization as a whole can learn and adapt.

Annie Howard, a consultant at Bain & Company, was intrigued by some of Scrum Inc.'s stories about Scrum at Bosch, so she decided to really dig into it and find out exactly what happened. Bosch makes everything from dishwashers to car safety systems to agricultural sensors to power tools. It employs hundreds of thousands of people. It is a big company. An old company too—they've been around since 1886. But what worked then, they realized, was not going to work in the twenty-first century. With the Internet of Things, they came to realize that every single thing they made would have to be connected to the Internet at some point. To keep up they needed to use Scrum. As Bosch CEO Volkmar Denner said in 2017, "For Bosch Agility is crucial. It allows us to respond to the increasing speed of change around us. Agility allows us to remain as an innovation leader."

Denner and his team decided to do what I mentioned above: create a dual organization. Anywhere they had to innovate, they would use Scrum; everywhere else could stay the same. But they realized quickly that to get the results they wanted, to become a truly Renaissance Enterprise, they needed to do it everywhere. Denner and his board decided to make the whole company Agile. They drew up a project plan, complete with Gantt charts. They were trying to implement Scrum using waterfall tools. And then they were surprised they weren't getting the results they wanted.

They decided to completely change themselves and how Bosch's steering committee ran itself. Denner and his board set themselves up as a Scrum Team. They had a Product Owner, a Scrum Master, in order to be cross-functional and drive change every single Sprint. They decided to have a common backlog for the entire organization of four hundred thousand people.

The steering committee no longer sat down at a long mahogany table as their underlings presented to them. They stood up. They walked around. They made the work visible on the walls. They realized that annual planning and funding locked them into the priorities they thought had been good a year earlier, and they needed to change faster. They moved to continuous planning and continuous funding cycles. *They reduced the cost of changing their minds.*

As the impediments and problems started bubbling up to the Executive Action Team, they realized something else as well: what they thought had been problems limited to one small part of their business, one limited silo, were actually endemic to the organization. They were able to see, for the first time, the whole system, rather than just focusing on the individual pieces.

They created a list of principles they would operate by and publicize within the company. They titled it "We Lead Bosch." Some of them are typical: "We live by our values" and "We achieve excellence." That could be the typical corporate pablum that every senior leadership team says they live by. But some of the rest of the list is really interesting:

- "We create autonomy and remove any obstacles."
- "We prioritize, keep things simple, make decisions quickly, and execute rigorously."
- "We learn from mistakes, and see them as part of our innovation culture."
- "We collaborate across functions, units, and hierarchies, always focused on results."

- "We seek and give feedback, and lead with Trust, Respect, and Empathy."

The results of all this? Well, they employed Scrum Teams for the groups at Bosch that worked with the electric car company Tesla. Tesla is an incredibly fast-paced company and demands the same of their partners. Using Scrum, Bosch cut its development time in half, adapting chassis and safety systems to get the kind of handling Tesla wanted. In their agriculture unit, a group of Teams is working on connected sensors to improve the growing of asparagus, of all things. These Teams produced ten innovations in four weeks, instead of their traditional one innovation over the course of six to eight months. Their home and garden unit has gone completely Agile. These are the folks who make power tools. And the Teams included everyone from designers to marketers—every skill needed to deliver a drill to market.

By setting up that Executive Action Team at the top, they were able to drive major change throughout a humongous company. It's not always easy, but the results can be remarkable.

The Executive Action Team

At Schlumberger, when they formed their Executive Action Team, their first impediment was their seating chart.

Imagine the complexity of taking an existing building with an existing org structure and rearranging more than 1,000 people in an existing floor plan. It's not easy. It takes time. But the Executive Action Team decided not to let it slow them down.

"We said, 'Let's just go with the seating plan we have. We'll fix it later,'" says Brady. "But that actually is the nature of Scrum. You go fast." Move quickly, track the impediments, but keep moving.

Another impediment they faced was a reluctance to make decisions. It was a pattern they set out to break. The people under them weren't used to it. It wasn't how they'd worked in the past. Impediments would flow up to the Executive Action Team that should have been handled at a lower level. So they pushed back. *Your Product Owner can make those decisions,* they said. They pushed responsibility out to the nodes. They focused on shortening their decision latency. There is no need to wait. Do.

The Product Owner Cycle

On the other side of that diagram, you have the organization that decides what to do. What should we build, deliver, provide, research? And how do we make sure that what we are building is what we actually want? How do we make sure that at the Team level we are building something that relates to our strategic vision? Those are questions the Product Owners need to answer.

One of our clients builds home automation systems. The heat and air-conditioning are talking to the doorbell, which is talking to the security system, which is talking to the lights. That kind of thing. So, at a high level, they had a vision for this whole product. But how could they cut down this huge thing into small enough pieces of work that could be finished by a Team in a week or two?

So we said, *Let's take the doorbell, for instance. There are a few Teams working on that, and one of those Teams is responsible for the camera. Maybe that Team has an optics expert that the other Teams don't. What's the first thing that Team needs to do? What's the smallest thing they can do that will create actual value in their first Sprint?*

They decided that the first thing the camera Team needed to do was to decide what kind of lens they were going to use. It would determine a whole bunch of things about the whole doorbell—how much light comes through, how big the casing has to be, and so on. So they started thinking about what they wanted in the lens.

Size? Picture quality? Price? Durability? Scratch resistance? At their Sprint Review they decided to have a competition. They got a bunch of different kinds of lenses—glass, crystal, plastic—and hooked them up to a cheap webcam attached to a computer so that the stakeholders they brought in to help make this decision could actually *see* the differences, understand the trade-offs, and make an informed decision. The Product Owner Team needs to have a vision, get that vision into something that can be done, reprioritize as they learn more, and get the product out the door. They may need to meet with stakeholders and other Product Owners to make sure everyone is aligned.

At Schlumberger, they say that alignment not just at the top of the organization but across every level and teamwork is critical. "It's absolutely essential," says Brady. Without the Executive Action Team and an executive-level Product Owner Team, he says, this would not have happened effectively, and Scrum would likely not have been as successful for Schlumberger.

The Art of the Possible

When your organization has done what Scrum makes possible—when you self-organize into going faster, raising quality, and responding quickly to an ever-changing world—you fundamentally shift the trajectory of your organization. Schlumberger's IT Team did. Eric Abecassis has the data to prove it. "Here we are, twice the work in half the time. We did even better than that."

"My intention," Eric says forcefully, "my mission is to generalize the concept of a 'Team of Teams' that is supported by the Scrum principles to become a tool to drive business." He pauses for a moment. "That's my vision. That's my ambition. And that's what I'm working at."

THE TAKEAWAY

Expect a fight before the renaissance. There will be resistance to change. You have to have a plan. You need to figure out a way to protect your Scrum Teams from the "institutional antibodies" that may try to attack them.

Scale Scrum using Scrum. Just as Scrum Teams self-organize and distribute the work, a network of Teams does the same thing. You want to push decisions out to those nodes on the edge, so you scale robustly. Because if one node goes down, it's not that big a deal. The system becomes self-healing, growing, responding, and changing as the environment does.

Scrum@Scale creates a known stable interface. Just as you want your products to be made up of loosely coupled components, you want your organization to be set up the same way. By having these known stable interfaces, you create a complex adaptive system that can learn and change as it grows. The "right" organization *emerges* through fast inspect and adapt cycles.

BACKLOG

- What impediments would you raise to an Executive Action Team in your organization? If you were on that Team, how would you remove those same impediments? What's stopping you from doing that now?

- Do managers in your organization have a clear and compelling vision for your products or services? Is it the right vision? Is it shared effectively and convincingly? How would you like to see it shared?

- Are you willing to change? To use Scrum? Are others in your organization willing? How would you stop the "institutional antibodies" from fighting a Scrum implementation?

- If you could redesign your workplace into a network of Teams, what would it look like?

CHAPTER 10

The Way the World Could Be

In the nineteenth century, the predominant theory of the spread of disease was known as the miasma theory. Basically, the idea was that decaying matter released "miasmata," or disease particles, that wafted through the air carrying disease. This bad air was thought to come out mainly at night.

This had been the prevailing theory of the spread of disease for *centuries*, going back to Roman times. And not just in Europe—India and China had similar theories of the spread of disease. The problem is, if you are wrong about the transmission vector of a disease, you defend against the *wrong* thing.

London, 1840s. The capital of the global British Empire. The empire on which the sun never sets and so forth. Being the center of government, finance, and the empire, combined with the advent of the industrial revolution, brought more and more people into London's crowded streets. And with them came disease. Sewers were often poorly planned and overflowing. Many houses had cesspools beneath them full of human waste that would leak out into the streets when it rained. It rains a lot in London.

People were crammed together in tight quarters. One of the most feared diseases was cholera. It killed thousands. London had major outbreaks in 1841, in 1849, and again in 1854. Dr. William Farr, at the time one of the most influential thinkers in public health, was convinced that the disease spread through the air from the dirty banks of the Thames into people's houses, striking them down. He studied the outbreaks carefully and came to the conclusion that there was an inverse correlation between elevation and cholera infections: if you lived on a hill, you were less likely to get cholera. It was obvious that it was the miasma, the bad air, that caused disease.

Dr. John Snow had a different point of view, one that was not common or accepted. Snow is an interesting figure, among other things he was a leader in the use of anesthesia in medicine, and one of the very first doctors to use it for women during childbirth, including for the birth of Queen Victoria's eighth and last child, Leopold.

Snow is also recognized as the father of modern epidemiology. He suspected that it wasn't miasmatic air that caused cholera, but some sort of contaminant in the water Londoners drank. In 1849, after a cholera outbreak that took nearly fifteen thousand lives, he wrote a paper, "On the Mode of Communication," which argued that water was the likely culprit. His theory was dismissed by medical authorities and the public.

When cholera broke out again in 1854, he quickly sprang into action, which he recounted in an updated 1855 version of his essay:

> The most terrible outbreak of cholera which ever occurred in this kingdom, is probably that which took place in Broad Street, Golden Square, and the adjoining streets, a few weeks ago. Within two hundred and fifty yards of the spot

where Cambridge Street joins Broad Street, there were upwards of five hundred fatal attacks of cholera in ten days. The mortality in this limited area probably equals any that was ever caused in this country, even by the plague; and it was much more sudden, as the greater number of cases terminated in a few hours.[1]

As bad as the Black Plague itself over a matter of hours.

On Broad Street (now Broadwick Street) there was a popular water pump. Snow suspected that there was something in the water from that pump that was so devastating the neighborhood. He went to the registrar and got a list of everyone who had died in the area, and the address of where they lived. As a result, he produced the map on page 230:

The little black rectangles indicate how many people died at that address. And then he started interviewing people about where they got their water. He found that nearly all the deaths occurred among people who lived close to the Broad Street pump. Only a handful of people who died in the outbreak lived closer to another pump. And the Broad Street pump was popular indeed.

> The water was used for mixing with spirits in all the public houses around. It was used likewise at dining-rooms and coffee-shops. The keeper of a coffee-shop in the neighborhood, which was frequented by mechanics, and where the pump-water was supplied at dinner time, informed me (on 6th September) that she was already aware of nine of her customers who were dead. The pump-water was also sold in various little shops, with a teaspoonful of effervescing powder in it, under the name of sherbet; and it may have been distributed in various other ways with which I am unacquainted.

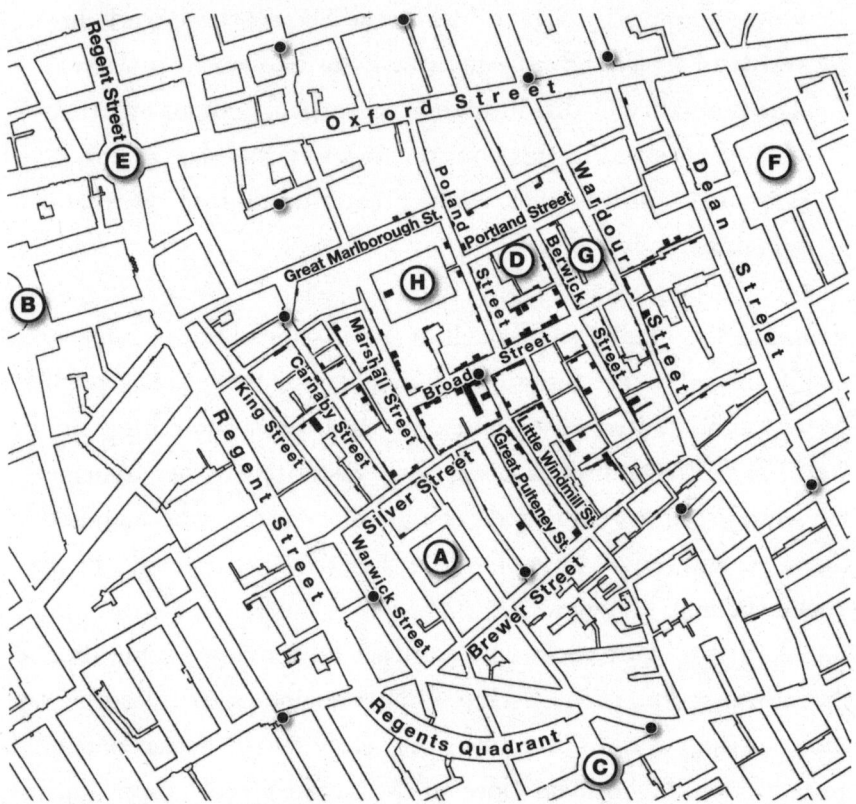

POINTS OF INTEREST			
A	Golden Square	E	Regent Circus
B	Hanover Square	F	Soho Square
C	Piccadilly Regent Circus	G	Wardour Mews
D	Portland Mews	H	Work House
•	Pumps		

And then there were the outliers. An elderly woman and her niece who lived in the West End died of cholera. There were no other cases of cholera in the neighborhood, and the woman hadn't been to Broad Street in months. But her son recalled that she loved the taste of the Broad Street water, and paid for a large bottle to be brought to her every day by a cart.

The water was taken on Thursday, 31st August, and she drank of it in the evening, and also on Friday. She was seized with cholera on the evening of the latter day, and died on Saturday . . . A niece, who was on a visit to this lady, also drank of the water; she returned to her residence, in a high and healthy part of Islington, was attacked with cholera, and died also. There was no cholera at the time, either at West End or in the neighborhood where the niece died.

Snow presented his findings to the local Board of Governors, and they had the handle to the Broad Street pump removed. Deaths immediately began to decrease. On further investigation it turned out that the public well had been dug just three feet from a cesspit that was seeping into the water. The culprit for the wave of death? Washing the diapers of a baby with cholera from another area.

It was the founding event of modern epidemiology, proving the germ theory of disease by using deduction from observable evidence and patterns. It changed how London dealt with its waste and water purity, right?

Nah. That took another cholera epidemic. Admitting that John Snow was right would've meant that all of the things the medical authorities had done over the years to protect the public were useless. They were right, and Snow was wrong, they insisted. So they put the pump handle back on after the epidemic subsided. It wasn't until 1866, eight years after John Snow's death, that Dr. Farr admitted that maybe, just maybe, Snow was right.

This kind of response frequently happens when a new way of thinking comes along, replacing the old way of doing things. Today the germ theory of disease is not only accepted but proven. We know for a fact that microscopic organisms of various types cause disease. We can look at them under microscopes, breed them, use them to immunize people. We know this to be true.

I started *The Scrum Fieldbook* with the story of Antoine Lavoisier and how he changed the world by saying that what had come before simply didn't make *sense*. New technologies allowed us to peer into the very building blocks of matter and see the system that organizes it. It was a fundamental shift in perspective: the world used to be one way, and then it was another. There would be no going back to the days of alchemy. Yes, there were debates and arguments and nasty letters to the editor for years, but eventually the system that actually worked won out. We take it for granted now, but not so long ago it was fiercely fought.

A Deduced Framework

Like John Snow, I'm not saying that practitioners of Scrum have all the answers, or even know all the questions, but I think we have enough evidence to reshape how we see things. We have enough patterns to deduce a general framework.

Scrum was developed and has grown exactly the same way as so many new discoveries. First, there were isolated pockets of success. Then some practices that worked over here, and something else that worked over there. We've continued to learn more over the years, discovering new things that work, new patterns. But they all come back to that simple, uncomplicated framework called Scrum.

And there has been resistance. People will still insist upon their Gantt charts and project plans and business requirements. They will hold on to their beliefs even in the face of the evidence. That is why I have given you examples of Scrum being used in all sorts of places to do all sorts of things. It simply is a better way of working.

A Better World

When I first began writing this book, I was appalled at the increasing polarization in the world, the fighting of old social and political battles to the death, the seeking to assign blame, the distrust of the other, be they your neighbor or someone far away. The world seemed a darker place somehow. Our ambition seemed weaker; we argued incessantly about small things instead of working together to solve big problems.

Now, I'm not holding my breath, but I like to think the work we do—helping people reach their full potential, helping organizations actually get things done, freeing up our tragically wasted human potential—can at least put a thumb on the scale for good.

Denmark, if you aren't aware, might just be the flattest country on the planet. It's home to Lego, Maersk (the largest shipping container company in the world), and the Carlsberg Group (which makes Carlsberg beer). They all use Scrum. Scrum has become so dominant in Denmark that it has become almost a default, especially in technology. "That's my gut feeling. Certainly in software. It's just how we work," says Carsten Jakobsen.

Carsten started perhaps the first Scrum transformation in Denmark at Systematic in 2006. Systematic makes software for healthcare, defense, intelligence, and national security, the kind of areas where people die if something goes wrong. Carsten was experimenting with four pilot projects and was moving them to an incremental, iterative approach when someone told him it was called Scrum. So he called Scrum Inc. to come train them all. Velocity doubled. Defects dropped 41 percent. And there were happy customers and happier Teams.

"It's the only time I've ever seen all those metrics improve at once," says Carsten. "Usually you try something and maybe one of those improves. Not all of them."

Over the next few years, Scrum spread throughout Systematic, eventually reaching the leadership level. The CEO was very data-driven, says Carsten, and when he saw the improvements the Teams were making, he implemented Scrum at the leadership level, requiring everyone to attend a Daily Scrum.

Since then Carsten has started his own company, Grow Beyond, and is also a lecturer at Aalborg University. He told me he was pretty sure that Scrum is being taught at every university in Denmark. And now he's working with older and more established companies—manufacturing, finance, insurance. He says that even traditional management is catching on now, and the reason is simple: companies are realizing that to be able to adapt to the pace of change, *they* must change. "It is do or die," he says. "If you change your company this way, you will survive. If not, you will die."

This is the refrain I hear over and over from executives. Every company has to start thinking like a technology company—the market is changing that quickly. They have to change or risk being outpaced and made irrelevant by a more nimble competitor.

I traveled to Japan last summer, when I had been invited by our partner KDDI to see how they have been building Scrum into what they do. KDDI, a large telecom in Japan, sees Scrum as a way to fundamentally shift the trajectory of Japan's economy.

Established as a regulated company in 1953, KDDI was the Japanese side of the first live television broadcast between Japan and the United States. They were the first to offer service on the thousands of miles of transpacific cables that connect the United States and Asia. They signed on early with Intelsat. After deregulation, they jumped into mobile, broadband, the whole nine yards. It is a big company. They've always seen themselves driving technology forward.

They brought Scrum Inc. over in 2016 so that they could use Scrum themselves. They recognize that as the Internet of Things and 5G become real, they need to develop services and devices for their customers rapidly. But they also brought us over to push Scrum into Japanese industry.

Japan is in an economic malaise and has been for decades: slow to no growth, foreign competition beating them out not only on price but also on innovation. It is also a very different culture than the one I'm used to. The smartest university graduates don't go into engineering, they go into management. They know if they get one of those coveted corporate or government jobs, they are set for life. No one ever gets fired. But those jobs aren't building new things or creating more innovation; they're about managing the people who manage the work. So most Japanese technology work is outsourced to contractors, to systems integrators. The companies have lost their ability to actually do just about anything.

Akihito Fujii is the person who brought us in. He has a remarkable path very different than most Japanese executives. He worked in the Japanese offices of Sun Microsystems and at Google but reported to management in the United States. He is steeped in the Silicon Valley mentality. And he liked the open and innovative atmosphere and mentality. But he saw something more. Something bigger. Not a company but a country that needed the same shift in mentality. So he launched an effort to help Japan.

"That way of working—incredible competition, creative destruction, the only thing that matters is success—that works well for me, J.J.," he told me. "But what about the other people? How are we going to help them too, not just me?"

So we traveled around Japan together speaking to groups of Japanese executives. The feeling and conversation were the same everywhere: *Japan is stuck in a rut. We must change our business culture if we are to save Japan.* They see Scrum as part of that effort. KDDI has built an incubator, KDDI Digital Gate, to train their engineers, suppliers, and customers on how to do Scrum and rapidly iterate on real products. It's remarkable.

But what stuck with me from the trip was the sense of hope. The sense that, working together, we can use Scrum to free up the paralysis that has seized Japanese businesses.

Increase Love with Use

Often today everything is put into transactional terms: *You do this for me, I'll do that for you.* It implies that there is a limited supply of everything, and that all interactions must be tallied up to see if things were fair or not. This sees life and choices as economic transactions. It's a very human approach. I have two young daughters, and believe me, I am lectured to about the importance of fairness often.

But there are certain things for which fairness and that kind of thinking don't really work. Is there a limited supply of good deeds one can do? Is there a limited supply of kindness? Does my joy diminish yours?

The late economist Albert O. Hirschman wondered about these things, pointing out that if love or public spirit are seen to be scarce resources that can be depleted, as things that can become rare, then parsimony is the logical response. But, he wrote,

> first of all, these are resources whose supply may well increase rather than decrease through use; second, these resources do not remain intact if they stay unused; like the ability to speak a foreign language or to play the piano, these moral resources are likely to become depleted and to atrophy if not used.[2]

A resource that becomes atrophied through disuse but grows through being used. If we transactionalize our support for one another, it dwindles; if we practice that support, it increases. Act the way you would like to be.

At this point we live in something of an atomized society. Things that the community used to provide, like childcare, or checking in on each other, or looking out for the elderly, have been outsourced to private entities. The care might even be better, but the community is weaker. We see ourselves as lone actors. And this makes us weaker as individuals. Because connection, real connection, matters. We even have the data.

One of my new favorite studies is innocently titled "Social Ties and Susceptibility to the Common Cold."[3] What these researchers did was take a couple of hundred people, see how lonely they were, and then, in a bit of experimental cruelty, exposed them to a cold virus. They first rated all of them on a social network index:

> These include relationships with a spouse, parents, parents-in-law, children, other close family members, close neighbors, friends, workmates, schoolmates, fellow volunteers (e.g., charity or community work), members of groups without religious affiliations (e.g., social, recreational, or professional), and members of religious groups. One point is assigned for each type of relationship (possible score of 12) for which respondents indicate that they speak (in person or on the phone) to someone in that relationship at least once every 2 weeks.[4]

Okay, I know you just did that too. I've got a score of 5. Hmmmm, maybe I should work on that. And guess what—the more connected you are, the less likely you are to get sick. People with fewer than three connections got a cold more than 60 percent of the time; those with four or five, a little over 40 percent of the time; and those with six or more, a little more than 30 percent. If you have six or more social roles you are half as likely to get sick as those with only three. And one study that followed nearly seven thousand adults for nine years found that the least socially connected people were more than *two times* as likely to die in that period as the most connected.[5] Being lonely will kill you.

Why is that? Well, there are a few reasons. The first is the idea of stress buffering. If you are faced with a stressful event, having a social network of support helps you deal with it. But it does so in an interesting way. What matters is not whether the support is really there but the *perception* that the support is there. That's right—even if you don't ask for help, just knowing that you can helps you. It actually keeps you alive. One seven-year study of Swedish men over fifty found that the ones who didn't have a high degree of perceived emotional support and experienced a number of stressful events—divorce, death of a loved one, losing a job, that kind of thing—were much more likely to die than those who did have a perception of support.[6]

And then there is the effect of the group. Of understood roles. Of understanding your place in the world. Sheldon Cohen of Carnegie Mellon wrote in a paper titled "Social Relationships and Health"—a paper cited nearly five thousand times—that understanding roles and norms in a group is a critical factor in mental and physical health:

> Role concepts that are shared among a group of people help to guide social interaction by providing a common set of expectations about how people should act in different roles. In meeting normative role expectations, individuals gain a sense of identity, predictability and stability; of purpose; and of meaning, belonging, security, and self-worth.[7]

Having a network of expected support. Having a common set of expectations on who does what and how to act in certain roles. Purpose. Meaning. Security. Self-worth. These are the things Scrum helps to create. It sets up a framework to give that to people daily. Because without that social connectedness, support, and common expectations, people suffer. They are diminished. Together we can move mountains and shake the pillars of heaven. Apart, we dwindle; we become less than what we are truly capable of becoming. Once you change your view of how the world works and see that the old axioms no longer apply, once you can do that, you can change what is possible—both for you and for the world. Scrum works in any place where humans come together. A mathematical truth is something that works in all possible universes, not just the one we happen to inhabit. Thus the statement $1+1=2$ is more fundamental than Newton's laws of motion or the law of gravity (both of which play a role in the prediction that the sun will come up tomorrow). On some worlds, where the rules of the universe are different, that may or may not happen. But mathematics remains unchanged and can describe those worlds too. Scrum is rooted in the way humans are, regardless of what language they speak or work they do. It is a fundamental tool for unleashing human possibility.

One of the exciting things about the human condition is the frequent discovery that the way you thought the world worked isn't, in fact, the way the world works. I love it when that happens. When I see the world anew.

THE TAKEAWAY

Decision time. The world, as you've seen, is changing. That can paralyze you or it can free you. What seems undoable can be done. I can't make you do it; I can only show you how. You have the tools, the tips, the path forward. The future is not fixed. Don't live in scarcity—live in abundance. The possibilities are limitless.

BACKLOG

- Go.

ACKNOWLEDGMENTS

Scrum, the millions of Scrum Teams across the planet, Scrum Inc., and this book itself would never have existed without my father's vision and passion for a better way of working. Thanks, Dad.

All great organizations are built on great Teams. I am privileged to work with some of the best. This book owes its life to the support, effort, generosity of spirit, and brilliance of them all. *The Clubhouse* is that stable of unicorns whose hard work, deep thinking, passion, and humanity are reflected in these pages. You truly are the best there has ever been. *The Sales Guild* is a Team that truly does twice the work in half the time, over and over and over again. You keep Scrum Inc. going. *Webside* is a group that pivots, turns, and overdelivers with such grace and joy I am astounded. You are the best Scrum Team I know of; you're pretty remarkable. *Markdom*, I sometimes nervously suspect you aren't totally kidding about world domination. Lastly, *Voyager*, the Team I am lucky enough to be a Team Member of, guards the spirit and guides the course of Scrum Inc. Thank you all.

Thanks to my fearless agent, Howard Yoon, and the Team at

RossYoon. Howard was the first person to tell me I could write a book and held my feet to the fire to get both of them to done. Anyone who is reading this should be grateful to him for making them better than they had any right to be.

Roger Scholl and his Team at Currency's belief in Scrum and hard work made this book as good as it is. I'll always admire how gently Roger pointed out that the first chapter was a piece of total garbage. He also gave me the critical insight that people already know how bad things are; I needed to give them the tools to work their way out.

Every time I read the acknowledgments at the back of a book, they always seem to talk about how writing is a lonely process. I'm not sure how anyone else does it, but the cross-functional Team that made this one a reality made it fun. @Citizen, the moment you came up with the closing line of the book is when I knew we'd done something remarkable. I only gently remind you that clothes do come in colors other than gray. @Rick, my partner in crime for all these years, we're actually pulling it off. And I don't care what you say—you owe me a hundred bucks because I'm totally right. @Tom, you've watched my back in more than one war and always remind me to get over myself. You, as always, just made shit happen during this whole process. You're still completely wrong about Elway, but I'll overlook it. @Veronica, it was you who corrected our course toward hope in this book. Your elegance of mind, sharpness of wit, and discernment of eye pulled on the threads and tied it all together. At the end it was you who did the final fine polish and caught the stupid mistakes. And, okay, the pistachios were totally your idea.

Anyway, tacos for everyone; they're on me.

And I'd like to thank my two amazing daughters, who put up with Papa being gone so much while I worked on this book, and greeted me with screaming joy every time I did enter the house. You make it all worthwhile.

Last, I'd like to thank all the AirBnB hosts on Capitol Hill. This book was written sporadically in your homes and basements over the course of a year. You know who you are. Five stars.

J. J. Sutherland
Washington, D.C.
March 24, 2019

NOTES

CHAPTER 1: THE CHOICE BEFORE US

1. Antoine-Laurent Lavoisier, *Elements of Chemistry*, trans. Robert Kerr (Edinburgh, 1790; facs. reprint, New York: Dover, 1965), xv–xvi.
2. https://www.standishgroup.com/sample_research_files/CHAOS Report2015-Final.pdf.

CHAPTER 3: WHY WE CAN'T DECIDE

1. Christopher Langton, in Roger Lewin, *Complexity: Life at the Edge of Chaos* (New York: Macmillan, 1990), 12.
2. From a speech to the National Defense Executive Reserve Conference in Washington, DC, November 14, 1957, in *Public Papers of the Presidents of the United States, Dwight D. Eisenhower* (Washington, DC: National Archives and Records Service, Government Printing Office, 1960), 5:818.

CHAPTER 4: BUSY VS. DONE

1. David Strayer, Frank Drews, and Dennis Crouch, "A Comparison of the Cell Phone Driver and the Drunk Driver," *Human Factors,* Summer 48.2 (2006): 381–391.

CHAPTER 5: PEOPLE AND PLACES THAT SEEM CRAZY USUALLY ARE

1. Peter Drucker, *Management: Tasks, Responsibilities, Practices* (1974; repr., New York: HarperCollins, 2009), 237.

CHAPTER 6: STRUCTURE IS CULTURE

1. Melvin E. Conway, "How Do Committees Invent," *Datamation*, April 1968.
2. Neil Garrett, Stephanie Lazzaro, Dan Ariely, and Tali Sharot, "The Brain Adapts to Dishonesty," *Nature Neuroscience* 19(2016): 1727–1732.

CHAPTER 7: DOING IT RIGHT

1. Jeff Sutherland, N. Harrison, and J. Riddle, IEEE HICSS 47th Hawaii International Conference on System Sciences, Big Island, Hawaii, 2014.
2. ScrumPLoP, *A Scrum Book: The Spirit of the Game* (Raleigh, NC: Pragmatic Bookshelf, 2019).
3. Ibid.
4. Bruce Tuckman, "Developmental Sequence in Small Groups," *Psychological Bulletin,* vol. 63, no. 6 (1965): 384–399.
5. Scrum PLoP, *A Scrum Book.*
6. Ibid.
7. Ibid.
8. Ibid.
9. Ibid.
10. Ibid.
11. Ibid.

CHAPTER 9: THE RENAISSANCE ENTERPRISE

1. Peter Drucker, *Innovation and Entrepreneurship* (1985; repr., New York: HarperCollins, 2009), 37.
2. Isaac Pino, "Why Autodesk Shares Are Surging Even as Sales Slide," The Motley Fool, May 3, 2018.

CHAPTER 10: THE WAY THE WORLD COULD BE

1. John Snow, *On the Mode of Communication of Cholera*, 2nd ed. (London: John Churchill, 1855).
2. Albert O. Hirschman, "Against Parsimony: Three Easy Ways of Complicating Some Categories of Economic Discourse," *Economics and Philosophy* 1 (1985): 7–21.
3. S. Cohen, W. J. Doyle, D. P. Skoner, B. S. Rabin, and J. M. Gwaltney Jr., "Social Ties and Susceptibility to the Common Cold," *Journal of the American Medical Association* 277 (1997): 1943.

4. Ibid.
5. L. F. Berkman and L. Syme, "Social Networks, Host Resistance, and Mortality: A Nine-Year Follow-Up Study of Alameda County Residents," *American Journal of Epidemiology* 109 (1979): 190.
6. A. Rosengren, K. Orth-Gomer, H. Wedel, and L. Wilhelmsen, "Stressful Life Events, Social Support, and Mortality in Men Born in 1933," *British Medical Journal* 307 (1993): 1104.
7. Sheldon Cohen, "Social Relationships and Health," *American Psychologist*, November 1994, 678–679.

INDEX

Abecassis, Eric, 207, 209–211, 224
Acceleration, 151
Adobe, 123, 124, 146
Affordable Care Act, 152
Afghanistan, 89
Agile, 11–14, 21, 36, 40–41, 51, 58, 72, 77, 96, 103, 109, 110, 120, 122, 124, 135, 146, 177, 216, 220, 222
Alexander, Christopher, 149–150
Alignment map, 198
Amazon, 61, 77, 146
American Ground: Rebuilding the World Trade Center (Langiewiesche), 64
American Revolution, 57
Amygdala, 89, 91, 111, 127
Anderson, Mark, 32–35
Antelo, Kim, 102–103, 142, 180–181, 201
Anti-patterns, 180–195, 205, 206
Apple, 76, 77, 146, 187
Arab Spring, 62, 88
Army Corps of Engineers, 64

Auld, Tom, 28–31
Autodesk, 216–217

Ba, 112, 158
Backlog Refinement, 25, 53–54, 192
Baggett, McCaul, 190
Bain & Company, 220
Ball, Kevin, 140–141
Beedle, Mike, 12
Bezos, Jeff, 95–96
Blame, culture of, 134, 135
Boeing, 76
Bonaparte, Napoleon, 65
Bosch, 11, 220–222
Brady, Jim, 210, 219, 222, 224
Burndown Chart, 171, 179, 197
Burton, Michael, 63–64
Business Requirement Documents (BRDs), 102, 103

California Department of Motor Vehicles, 18
Cargo Cult Scrum, 188, 190
Carlsberg Group, 233

INDEX

Cellular automata, 55, 56
Change, rate of, 5–6
Change Control Boards, 31
CHAOS Report, 40
Chemistry, 3–4
Cholera, 228–231
Coca Cola, 11
Cohen, Sheldon, 238
Collocation, 204
Commitment, as Scrum value, 129–130
Complex adaptive systems, 55–56, 66, 105, 145
Confirmation bias, 107
Confirmation.com, 68–70, 73, 74, 79, 84
Connecting for Health, 18
Connection, 84, 112–114, 115, 116
Connection (radio show), 155–156
Context switching loss, 83
Conway, Melvin, 119
Conway's law, 119, 120, 164, 216
Courage, as Scrum value, 135–136, 147
Craziness, 87–116
Culture (*see* Structure)
Cunningham, Ward, 13
Cynefin framework, 60, 62
Cynicism, Voice of, 109–110, 116

Daily Scrum (Standup), 24, 34–35, 37, 53, 65, 133, 139, 192, 204, 212, 234
Daukas, Steve, 80–82
Decision latency, 42
Decision-making, 40–49, 59–60, 66, 124
Decision quadrant, 39
Dedicated Teams, 203
Deloitte, 96
Deming, W. Edwards, 111
Denmark, 233–234
Denner, Volkmar, 220
Dependencies, 30

Design and Construction, Department of (DDC), 63–64
Deterministic chaos, 59
"Developmental Sequence in Small Groups" (Tuckman), 156–157
DevOps, 182
Dibbits, Taco, 121, 122
Digital transformations, 11
Disease, spread of, 227–232
Done, definition of, 75, 77, 85, 86, 204
Drucker, Peter, 111, 210
Drummond Company, 137–138
Duke University, 127

Einstein, Albert, 42
Eisenhower, Dwight D., 39, 59, 62
Ek, Daniel, 77
Emails, 83–84
Emergency Procedure, 171–172, 176, 178
Enron, 102
Enterprise Resource Planning systems (ERPs), 16, 209
EODMU2 (Explosive Ordnance Disposal Mobile Unit 2), 50–54
Epidemiology, 228, 231
Estimation Points, 160
Executive Action Team, 137–139, 219–223, 226
Expeditionary Combat Support System, 18

Farr, William, 228, 231
Fear, 84, 87, 89, 91, 93, 107, 108, 110–112, 115, 116, 134
Federal Emergency Management Agency (FEMA), 64
Fidelity, 11
Flashbulb memories, 91
Focus, as Scrum value, 130–131
Forbes magazine, 95
Fowler, Martin, 12

INDEX

Fox, Brian, 68, 70
Frazee, David, 153, 154, 159, 161, 172
Frontal cortex, 106
"Frum, John," 188–189
Fujii, Akihito, 235
Functional silos, 99, 109, 110, 120
Furuhjelm, Jorgen, 10

Gantt chart, 33, 37, 220, 232
Garcia, Alberto, 138–139
Garcia Navarro, Lourdes, 88
General Electric Company, 96
General Relativity Theory, 42
Germ theory of disease, 231
Giuliani, Rudolph, 64
Good Housekeeping pattern, 168–170, 176, 178, 204
Google, 61, 71, 77, 146, 216, 235
Grande Armée, 65
Gravity, law of, 239
Grow Beyond, 234

Haase, Jon, 49–54
Hammer, Michael, 218
Happiest Company to Work For, The (Yamada), 47
Happiness metric, 175–176, 178, 179, 214
Harvard Business School, 119
Heitz, Hugo, 173
Hershman, Lisa, 218
Hirschman, Albert O., 238
Histoire de France (Michelet), 218
Holden, Kenneth, 63–64
House remodeling, 28–31
Howard, Annie, 220
Humphrey's law, 26, 31, 37
Hurricanes, 99

Impediment board, 194–195
Intelsat, 234
International Classification of Disease, 153–154

Internet of Things, 220, 234
Interrupt Buffer, 166, 167, 176, 178, 204
Interrupt pattern, 165, 167
iPhone, 25, 186–187, 196

Jakobsen, Carsten, 233–234
Johnson, Jim, 40–43, 45, 46
Johnson Controls, 32
Judgment, Voice of, 107–108, 116
Justice, Joe, 22, 77, 200

Kaikaku, 186
Kaizen, 173–174, 178, 186, 190, 204
KDDI, 234–236
KDDI Digital Gate, 235
Kemp, Chris, 75–77
Kernis, Jay, 101

Langiewiesche, William, 64
Langton, Christopher, 55, 56, 59
Lavoisier, Antoine, 3–5, 232
Leadership, 123–126, 147, 205
Lean Enterprise Institute, 185–187
Lego, 233
Libya, 87–89
Lightweight, 12
Lockheed Martin, 11
London Stock Exchange, 14–15, 17
Lying, 126–128, 134, 161

Madness (*see* Craziness)
Maersk, 233
Mariti, Riccardo, 117–118, 124, 129–130, 132–135, 146
Markem Imaje, 211–213
Massachusetts Institute of Technology (MIT), 27, 119
McRae, Hamish, 15, 17
Meetings, 45–46, 67, 93, 94
Memory, 89–91, 158
Mergers and acquisitions, 32–35
Miasma theory, 227

INDEX

Michelet, Jules, 218
Michener, James, 188
Microsoft, 119, 131
Middle management, change and, 144–145
Minimum viable bureaucracy, 136–140
Mirai Industry Company, 47–48
Moore, Gordon, 5
Moore's law, 5, 8, 14
Moran, Daniel Keys, 152
Motley Fool, The, 218
Muda, mura, muri, 162, 178, 179
Multitasking, 83, 84, 162
Musk, Elon, 76

National Health System, 18
National Highway Transportation Safety Administration, 83
National Public Radio (NPR), 87–89, 100–101
Nemawashi, 43
New Hebrides, 188
Newton's laws of motion, 239
No, importance of, 79–82, 84, 85, 95, 161
Nokia Mobile, 25, 196–197
Nonaka, Ikujiro, 112–113, 158

Office Connections, 150
Office of Emergency Management, 63
Ohno, Taiichi, 133, 162–163
"On the Mode of Communication" (Snow), 228
Openness, as Scrum value, 131–134, 147
OpenView Venture Partners, 151
Organizational debt, 139, 148, 185–187
Out of the Crisis (Deming), 111
Outcomes vs. outputs, 73–74, 82, 85, 86, 152
Outsourcing, 193, 205

PatientKeeper, 181–183
Pattern Language, A: Towns, Buildings, Construction (Alexander), 149–150
Patterns, 149–152, 155, 163, 165, 176–180
Peregrine Financial Group, 68
Performance review, 141–143
Phelps, Elizabeth, 90–91
Place to Wait, A, 150
Planning, 59, 62
Priorities, 70–73, 78, 79, 81, 84–86, 154, 201–203, 221
Problem types, 60–62
Process Efficiency, 200
Product Backlog, 23, 24, 26, 34, 37, 75, 82, 85, 103, 162
Product Owner (PO), 23–26, 28, 30, 34, 37, 45, 51, 59, 65, 82, 94–95, 103, 124, 142–143, 146, 166, 182, 187, 190, 192, 195–198, 201, 214, 219, 220, 223–224

Qaddafi, Muammer, 88

Rally, 159
Red River Army Depot, Texarkana, Texas, 168–171
Renaissance Enterprise, 8, 193, 207–226
Respect, as Scrum value, 134–135
Riccardo's Restaurant, London, 117–118, 124, 129–130, 132–135
Rigby, Darrell, 118–119, 122
Rijksmuseum, Netherlands, 121–123, 146
Ringi, 43–45, 47
Risk committee, 48
Roach, Patrick, 196

Saab Aerospace, 8–11, 139, 215, 216
SAAS (Software As A Service), 217

Samsung, 76
San Francisco Chronicle, 18
SAP, 16, 209–210
Sarbanes Oxley Act of 2002, 102, 103
Scaled Daily Scrum, 130
Scharmer, Otto, 107, 109, 110, 116
Schlumberger, 11, 207–210, 213, 216, 219, 222, 224
Schlumberger, Conrad, 208
Schlumberger, Marcel, 208
Schneier, Avi, 73, 79
Schwaber, Ken, 12
Schwartz, Fabian, 137–138
Scientific American, 91
Scott Safety, 32–34
Scrum
    Agile, 11–14, 21, 36, 40–41, 51, 58, 72, 77, 96, 103, 109, 110, 120, 122, 124, 135, 146, 177, 216, 220
    basics of, 23–37
    Daily Scrum (Standup), 24, 34–35, 37, 53, 65, 133, 139, 192, 203, 212, 234
    examples of, 28–36
    Executive Action Team, 137–139, 219, 221–224, 226
    five values of, 128–136, 148
    invention of, 12
    power of, 7, 10
    Product Owner (PO), 23–26, 28, 30, 34, 37, 45, 51, 59, 65, 82, 94–95, 103, 124, 142–143, 146, 166, 182, 187, 190, 192, 195–198, 201, 214, 219, 220, 223, 224
    Scrum@Scale, 9, 215, 218, 219, 225
    Scrum Master, 23, 24–25, 28, 37, 51, 124, 139, 142, 143, 146, 182, 189–190, 192, 194
    Scrum Master Cycle, 219–222

Scrum Pattern Language Project, 151
Scrum Teams, 7–10, 23–31, 34, 37, 45, 51, 58, 59, 65, 73, 79, 81, 82, 94, 97, 105, 113, 120, 129–130, 132–134, 138, 139, 142, 143, 151, 154–167, 172–174, 177, 184–185, 187–192, 196–198, 200–204, 211, 213–215, 222, 225
Scrumming the Scrum, 172–174, 176, 178
Sprint Backlog, 24, 25, 37, 130, 160–161, 163, 166, 171
Sprint Burndown Chart, 171
Sprint Planning, 24, 37, 53, 166, 192
Sprint Retrospective, 28, 35, 37, 52–54, 136, 138, 173, 175, 178
Sprint Review, 26–30, 37, 54, 94, 123, 166, 192, 224
Sprints, 23, 34, 37, 53–54, 73, 79, 146, 164, 204, 214
Stable Teams, 146, 178, 203
Velocity, 25, 27, 51, 73, 79, 142, 151, 155, 161, 176, 179, 190, 200, 202, 203, 214, 233
Scrum: The Art of Doing Twice the Work in Half the Time (Sutherland and Sutherland), 5, 18, 51, 153, 175, 184
Scrum Inc., 72, 73, 77, 80, 94, 95, 108, 113, 118, 133, 140, 142, 151, 165, 173, 176, 180–184, 192, 193, 196, 198, 207, 210, 212, 213, 220, 233, 234
September 11, 2001, terrorist attacks, 63–64, 90–91
Shalloway, Al, 119
Shalloway's corollary, 119
Sheive, Alex, 79, 165
Siemens, 103–104

Sisk, Jacob, 120–121, 125
Slack, 113
Slaten, Dave, 198–199
Snow, John, 228, 231, 232
Snowden, Dave, 60
"Social Relationships and Health" (Cohen), 238
"Social Ties and Susceptibility to the Common Cold" (Cohen, Doyle, Skoner, Rabin, Gwaltney Jr.), 237
Soviet Union, 56
Space X, 76
Sparrow, Tammy, 153–155, 160, 161, 164, 172, 174, 176–177
Spotify, 77–78
Sprint Backlog, 24, 25, 37, 130, 160–161, 163, 166, 171
Sprint Burndown Chart, 171
Sprint Planning, 24, 37, 53, 166, 192
Sprint Retrospective, 28, 35, 37, 52–54, 136, 138, 173, 175, 178
Sprint Review, 26–30, 37, 54, 94, 123, 166, 192, 224
Sprints, 23, 34, 37, 53–54, 73, 79, 146, 164, 203, 210, 214
Stable Teams, 146, 155–160, 176, 178, 203
Standish Group, 15, 36, 40, 42, 46, 72
Stealth Space Company, 75–78, 84
Storm time, 99–100, 115
Street Cafe, 150
Street Windows, 150
Stress buffering, 238
Strong, Arnold, 89
Structure, 117–123, 137, 139–140, 145, 147, 148
Subject matter experts (SMEs), 213
Sullivan, Chris, 212–213
Sun Microsystems, 235
Support networks, 236–239

Sutherland, Jeff, 5, 12, 18, 19, 24–25, 27, 56, 151, 153, 170, 171, 173, 181–183
Swarming patterns, 163–164, 176, 178, 204
Sweden, 8–11
Systematic, 233–234

Tales of the South Pacific (Michener), 188
Talisman system, 14
Tanna, 188–189
TAURUS project, 14–18
Team Happiness, 52, 53, 142
Team Member (*see* Scrum Teams)
Team Velocity, 51, 52
Teams That Finish Early Accelerate Faster pattern, 155, 176, 178
Tesla, 222
Texting, 83–84
3M Corporation, 31–36
3M Health Information Systems, 152–154, 159–161, 164, 167, 172, 174, 176
Timeboxing, 52
Timm, Heather, 133
Toyota Production System, 133, 162–163, 169, 170, 185, 186
Traffic, 56
Trait élémentaire de chimie (Elements of Chemistry) (Lavoisier), 3–4
Transparency, 131, 132, 134, 144, 147, 176, 202
Tuckman, Bruce, 156–157
Twitch, 61
Tyco International, 102

U.S. Securities and Exchange Commission (SEC), 102
U.S. Special Forces, 50
University College London, 127
University of Maryland, 119

Uriarte, Alexandra, 213
USAA, 11

Values (*see* Scrum, five values of)
Vanuatu, 188
Velocity, 25, 27, 51, 73, 79, 142, 151, 155, 161, 176, 179, 190, 200, 202, 203, 214, 233
Virgin Galactic, 76
Vision, 125–126

Wassendorf, Russell, Sr., 68–69
Waste, taxonomy of, 162–163, 178, 179

Waterfall systems, 33, 37, 120, 183, 220
Waterloo, Battle of, 57
WBUR Radio Station, Boston, 155–156
Well logging, 208
Wellesley, Arthur, Duke of Wellington, 57
World Health Organization, 153
WorldCom, 102

Yamada, Akio, 47
Yesterday's Weather, 160–161, 176, 178, 203, 214

ABOUT THE AUTHOR

J. J. Sutherland is the CEO of Scrum Inc., the leading provider of Scrum training and consulting worldwide. J.J. has personally trained thousands of people and helped companies large and small accelerate innovation, quickly adapt, and see their own capability to change the world they live in. He is the co-author of *Scrum: The Art of Doing Twice the Work in Half the Time*.

Before joining Scrum Inc., J.J. was an award-winning correspondent and producer with NPR. He covered stories from such places as Iraq, Afghanistan, Lebanon, Libya, and Egypt, as well as the aftermath of the Japanese tsunami of 2011. He has won duPont, Peabody, Edward R. Murrow, and Lowell Thomas awards for his work.

In his free time, J.J. enjoys cooking complicated recipes, traveling to the four corners of the globe, and gaming. He is also the co-host of the videogame review podcast *Only a Game* with Chris Suellentrop.

J.J. lives in Washington, D.C., with his wife and their two daughters.

ABOUT THE TYPE

This book was set in Perpetua, a typeface designed by the English artist Eric Gill (1882–1940), and cut by the Monotype Corporation between 1928 and 1930. Perpetua is a contemporary face of original design, without any direct historical antecedents. The shapes of the roman letters are derived from the techniques of stonecutting. The larger display sizes are extremely elegant and form a most distinguished series of inscriptional letters.